**THE 22 PRINCIPLES OF SUCCESS** SERIES – PART 1

# THE 8 PRINCIPLES OF ACHIEVEMENT, LOVE AND HAPPINESS

*How to get what you want and enjoy the process*

**PIP McKAY**

Published by
UNICORN PRESS
THE MAGIC OF TRANSFORMATION

Copyright © Pip McKay 2016
First Edition Jan 2016, Second Edition Sep 2016, Third Edition March 1017, Fourth Edition May 2018, Fifth Edition Jan 2019

This book is copyright. Apart from any fair dealing for the purposes of private study research, criticism or review, as permitted under the Australian Copyright Act 1968, no part may be reproduced by any process without written permission from the author. Every effort has been made to provide accurate and authoritative information in this book. Neither the publisher nor the author accepts any liability for injury, loss or damage caused to any person acting as a result of information in this book nor for any errors or omissions. Readers are advised that this book is not meant to replace or be instead of any counseling, psychology or psychiatric advice and if a reader needs this support to obtain advise from a licensed professional before acting on information provided in this book.

National Library of Australia Cataloguing-in-Publication

Creator: McKay, Pip, author.
Title: The 8 principles of achievement, love and happiness : how to get what you want and enjoy the process / Pip McKay
ISBN: 9780994446718 (hardback)
ISBN: 9780994446701 (paperback)
Subjects: Self-actualization (Psychology)
    Success.
    Happiness.
    Love.
    Mind and body.
    Leadership.
    Self-help techniques.
Design: Kylie Maxwell, ePrintDesign
Illustrator of goblet icon: Laila Savolainen
Dewey Number: 153.8
Printed & Channel Distribution
Lightning Source | Ingram (USA/UK/EUROPE/AUS)

"To my wonderful, inspiring mother, Elaine McKay, who has always encouraged my ideas and to my incredibly supportive partner, Will."

# CONTENTS

**Foreword 1 –**
Dale Beaumont, Founder of Business Blueprint ...... 6

**Foreword 2 –**
Eloise King, Founder of Soul Sessions ...... 9

**Introduction –**
What Are The 8 Principles? ...... 14

My Personal Journey with The 8 Principles ...... 17

Outline of The 8 Principles of
Achievement, Love and Happiness ...... 22

Importance of the Order of The Principles ...... 24

Where do The 8 Principles come from? ...... 26

**Section 1 –**
**The 8 Principles of Achievement, Love and Happiness** ...... 31

Chapter 1 – The Principle of Energy ...... 33

Chapter 2 – The Principle of Concentration ...... 41

Chapter 3 – The Principle of Receptivity ...... 51

Chapter 4 – The Principle of Creativity ...... 61

Chapter 5 – The Principle of Organisation ...... 71

Chapter 6 – The Principle of Intuition ...... 81

Chapter 7 – The Principle of Discernment ...... 91

Chapter 8 – The Principle of Results ...... 101

**Section 2 –
Understanding your Journey to
Successful Achievement** ...117

Four Stages Of Growth ...119

Stage 1 – Childhood – the Hero's Journey Begins ...124

Stage 2 – Adolescence – Crossing the First Threshold ...127

Stage 3 – Young Adult – Crossing the Second Threshold ...134

Stage 4 – Mature Adult – Crossing the Third Threshold ...139

**Section 3 –
Archetypal Story of the Hero's Journey to
the Ultimate Achievement** ...143

Parzival and the Holy Grail and His Stages of Growth ...145

Stage 1 – Childhood – Parzival's Journey Begins ...146

Stage 2 – Adolescence – Parzival Crosses the First Threshold ...154

Stage 3 – Young Adult – Parzival Crosses the Second Threshold 173

Stage 4 – Mature Adult – Parzival Crosses the Third Threshold ...180

**Bibliography** ...183

**About Pip McKay** ...185

## FOREWORD 1

# Dale Beaumont
## Founder of Business Blueprint

In 1997 I was sitting in a classroom surrounded by bored 16 year olds. I had enrolled in an accelerated learning course because there seemed so much to learn. But by the time the first class came around I wondered what I was doing there. Did I really want to spend my Saturday mornings in a classroom? Didn't I do enough of that at school?

Then Pip McKay walked into the room. She immediately engaged us all with her passion for the subject and the practical tools she taught. I couldn't believe how easy and fun it was to learn and how quickly it had an impact on my life. Pip gave me a model for effective learning and the tools and coaching to approach it in a whole new way.

Later when I was 19, I was working in an organisation that taught strategies for success. A number of the team had been inspired to learn Neuro-Linguistic Programming (NLP) to enhance performance and productivity, and who had they found to teach the course? Well it was Pip McKay, what a great piece of synchronicity! I knew I was in for an incredible experience and couldn't wait to begin.

What I learnt from Pip's unique approach to NLP opened me up to a whole new way of being. She taught me about success mindset, communication and how to clear negative beliefs and emotions. These skills had a profound impact on the way I thought and I still use them today. I was also able to apply many of those skills to sales and marketing and they have been extremely valuable to me in business as well. Since then Pip and I have remained in contact and I asked her to contribute to my *Secrets to Great Success Coaches Exposed* book that became a number one best seller.

One of the things I have seen in working with thousands of business owners is that you can have all the know-how in the world, you can have the best business strategies possible and be taught the latest developments in technology but if you don't have the right mindset and emotional wellbeing you are just not going to apply those skills and take the appropriate action. When I founded Business Blueprint I wanted to make sure that people who came to our conferences had the best business strategies possible and the best mindset to accompany it.

So it didn't take me long to invite Pip to be a regular speaker because I knew she could help people accelerate their results with her fresh, creative and profound approach. I have often heard people say Pip changed their lives, and this is after a forty-five minute speech, let alone those who go on to do her longer courses or do personal coaching with her. I recommend my clients to her because I know from my personal experience how valuable her insights are.

Pip really is a pioneer in the field of Personal Development and Transformational Coaching. She has a unique ability to find innovative solutions to the problems we all face and the resources to accelerate success. So with that in mind it was very exciting to see Pip's new offering, *The 8 Principles of Achievement, Love and Happiness*. In it Pip provides a blueprint of the internal resources you need to get what you want and feel happy and fulfilled in the process.

In business and personally, people face many problems they don't like to talk about. People get stuck, feel frustrated and even sabotage their success. Finding effective strategies to deal with negative thoughts and emotions is absolutely essential for success and happiness. Pip's work does exactly that. She is able to discover the real cause of internal problems and create effective and fast solutions. She is able to identify the gaps in people's resources and supply them with groundbreaking tools to support their success.

Now some eighteen years after I first met Pip, I have participated in hundreds of trainings, read countless books and interviewed some of the great leaders of our time. This gives me an even greater appreciation of Pip's wisdom and her ability to communicate it in a way that affects our very DNA. Her work always offers something special – something deeper, more intuitive and of great profundity.

I have often wondered what gave her that unique point of difference. In this book Pip outlines the principles that form the very foundation of her work and gives it that extra dimension and insight. *The 8 Principles of Achievement, Love and Happiness* gives you the mindset and emotional tools to accelerate your success. With these tools you have a systematic way of identifying problems and practical tools to overcome them so you can get back into flow.

Pip writes in the same way she presents – full of passion, insight and a sparkling sense of fun. She supports her wisdom with entertaining and thought provoking stories and examples, which make learning easy and more intuitive. It is a book you can read over and over again and gain greater insights each time.

I am excited that with the launch of this book – and Business Blueprints new TV channel, where Pip has her own show – her inspiring work will find an even greater audience. I look forward to many more years of knowing Pip and to hearing your stories of success and happiness.

**Dale Beaumont**
*Founder of Business Blueprint*
*Founder of Bizversity*
*Author of 16 best selling books*
*www.businessblueprint.com.au*

**FOREWORD 2**

# Eloise King
## Founder of Soul Sessions

Pip is one of the world's keepers of profound ancient knowledge. She holds wisdom that few people have access to. Her approach to life, personal and spiritual development is one of the most unique I have ever come across.

That is really saying something because I have spent most of my life, first as a journalist and now as the founder of *Soul Sessions*, interviewing some of the world's most famous luminaries, people such as Deepak Chopra, Wayne Dyer and Anita Moorjani. Pip's work is right up there with the best of them.

Pip is the next Joseph Campbell and instead of *The Hero with a Thousand Faces*, *The 8 Principles of Achievement, Love and Happiness* show us the eight faces of the soul and how to reveal them and make them real in our world.

Like many masterful teachers I heard about Pip McKay long before I met her. I knew she had spent twenty-two years of her life in a spiritual apprenticeship studying the Western Mystery Traditions, a type of spiritual education that is lost to most of us in the modern age.

I knew a number of Pip's coaching clients really well and saw incredible, magical, transformation in their lives. It was as if they had gone on some kind of archetypal Hero's Journey and returned truer to themselves, more passionate about life and more able to achieve what they wanted. It was as if a deep part of them had been healed and they had gained great clarity about their true purpose.

The stories emerging from her clients also involved archetypal figures that, in themselves, were incredibly alluring. It was as if they were inviting me to lean in and sip from their cup of wisdom.

When I later met Pip in her home for the first time, I felt like I'd been invited to dine at the Grail Castle where something magical would occur. Over a beautiful roast chicken and a little organic wine (on my side, Pip doesn't drink), our conversation flowed around great Renaissance art, modern NLP, Greek mythology, the Holy Grail and even the symbolic meaning of the Griffin.

Our conversation often returned to Pip's greatest passion – her profound knowledge of The 8 Principles and the archetypal figures that surround them. We discussed archetypal concepts such as Mother and Father and how these can help heal childhood wounds and discover our unique passion, purpose and talents.

Even though these topics may sound weighty they were all discussed with Pip's signature bubbly warmth. She is so full of life and I was touched by the lightness of her spirit and her passion.

Soon after, we were honoured to have her present on the *Soul Sessions* stage. It was an opportunity to record her brilliance for safe keeping in our video library of wisdom…alongside contributions from Neale Donald Walsch, and Dr Joe Dispenza, as well as, those mentioned before: Deepak Chopra, Wayne Dyer, Anita Moorjani and many more great teachers.

We all agree that knowledge is a wonderful thing, but masters like Pip have the ability to distill it down into digestible pieces so the rest of us can access it for positive results.

This book is exactly that.

When Pip asked me to write this foreword, I felt both honoured and excited. Honoured to be contributing in this very small way to a body of work that I knew was reflective of a lifetime of committed experience.

I felt excited because the timing for me could not have been more perfect. I was in need of guidance around a personal challenge that had me struggling to achieve an important business goal.

After many experiences of success in this area, suddenly every time I took a familiar step forward, another challenge would arise and a proverbial door would close. I couldn't make sense of what was going on so I soldiered on, but I was beginning to lose my way.

So, with the same eagerness I felt about meeting Pip for dinner, I awaited the arrival of her manuscript that is now this book. When it popped into the post box, life had organised itself so that I had two full days to just sit down and absorb its pages.

In the opening pages, Pip states: "If you're not getting what you want then one of these 8 Principles has not been fulfilled and its corresponding Secret has not been realised."

With that in mind I eagerly read *The 8 Principles* keen to see what I was missing. As I read each chapter on Energy, Concentration, Receptivity, Creativity, Organisation, Intuition, Discernment and Results they gave me a solid framework to analyse my challenge from a fresh perspective. In doing so I could identify the missing piece in my puzzling situation. It was all about the Principle of Energy.

"The secret to energy is inspiration," Pip writes. I realised then and there I had lost my inspiration for the thing I'd done so many times before. Without the right energy and inspiration, my results were stagnating and the rest of the principles were almost impossible to apply.

This new awareness empowered me to stop what I was doing and make a better choice right in that moment. It also reinforced for me that whatever I choose, it must always feel good, inspire me and be true for my soul's higher purpose. Since then the results have been amazing and my business has been rejuvenated.

I wonder which principle will hold the most power for you?

It is said that when the student is ready the teacher will appear. If you're holding this book in your hands, then I have no doubt it has the answers you've been searching for.

**Eloise King**
*Soul Sessions Founder*
*Mind, Body, Soul Journalist*
*www.SoulSessions.co*

## INTRODUCTION

# Outline of the 8 Principles of Achievement, Love and Happiness

### MY JOURNEY
### WHERE THE PRINCIPLES ORIGINATED

## INTRODUCTION

# WHAT ARE THE 8 PRINCIPLES?

For thousands of years people have wondered, what makes one person successful while others fail? What makes one person happy and fulfilled while others feel depressed and dissatisfied? What makes someone loveable and loving while others spend their lives alone? What makes someone special while others wallow in mediocrity?

What is that magical point of difference?

*The 8 Principles of Achievement, Love and Happiness* outlines the exact strategies that create success and wellbeing whatever they are for you. These principles are a step-by-step approach to getting what you want. If you're not getting what you want then one of The 8 Principles has not been fulfilled and its corresponding Secret has not been realised.

Some people stumble upon these tools intuitively and once they have them their world seems to open up, but this may take years of trial and error. Others stumble around in the dark, never really making the breakthrough and continually hitting their heads against figurative brick walls.

*The 8 Principles of Achievement, Love and Happiness* gives you all the tools you need to understand, apply and achieve what you want in life. It is a blueprint for results and fulfillment and outlines the Archetypal Journey to success. When things are not going the way you want them to, one of these 8 Principles is missing or being used incorrectly. When all 8 Principles are functioning effectively they become one of the pathways to enlightenment. Most people however don't have such lofty ideals – they just want to stop the frustration of not getting what they want or not being able to heal an area of their life that continues to trouble them.

Of course, like any principle, they have to be applied to work, so provided in the pages of this book are practical tools and activities you can use to improve the quality of every area of your life. This book is divided into three sections:. The first section is a practical guide to The 8 Principles with famous examples, client examples and personal examples along with exercises and processes to help you embody each principle. The second section is an outline of the Stages of Growth we need to move through in order to apply The Principles successfully to our own personal Hero's Journey. The third section is the most famous archetypal story of the knight Parzival, on his quest for the Holy Grail. This story is adapted from an extraordinary book written in the 12th Century called *Parzival and the Stone from Heaven.*

I have included this final section because stories talk to the deepest part of the subconscious mind and help us identify with the Hero and intuitively learn his lessons. This helps us to embed the resources of the first two sections making it easier to automatically access *The 8 Principles of Achievement, Love and Happiness.* All of us search for our own Holy Grail and this means different things to different people but in the end the most precious Grail is who we become in the journey of our development. If you wish you can read the story first and then come back to The 8 Principles. Or like most people you can read The 8 Principles first and then embed the learnings with the story. You can choose which way is right for you.

*The 8 Principles of Achievement* can be applied with equal success to your career, love life, health and happiness. As you read the book think about which area of your life would be the biggest Holy Grail of achievement for you at this moment in time. This helps to make the lesson practical and relevant to your personal situation. Each chapter has different examples outlined to assist you in this process.

The 8 Principles are the ultimate personal development tools. Sometimes, as I am sure you are aware, we cannot know what we don't know and may not realise what is holding us back.

With the 8 Principles you can feel assured that the answer is under one of these headings because The 8 Principles covers all the ways we are conscious and functional in our world in order to achieve. So whether your problem has a deep unconscious source or is something you have been aware of but just cannot shift the answer is here in these pages.

I know this because applying The 8 Principles has been a lifelong journey for me and made a massive difference to every area of my life. A warning however The 8 Principles will not stop you from having any problems – problems are necessary for our growth. What they do, instead, is make solving your problems much easier and they ensure that future problems are part of the pathway to your success and not a repeated pattern that will not shift.

# MY PERSONAL JOURNEY WITH THE 8 PRINCIPLES

I first came across The 8 Principles when I was nineteen years old. At the time I was severely depressed. Even though I was so young I had a sense that life had not turned out the way I wanted it to. Life felt purposeless and meaningless.

I felt lost and alone even though I was surrounded by people and I didn't really know what I wanted to do.

I had experienced childhood abuse from a family 'friend' from the age of about four until I was eight years old, and then went through a subsequent court case. Not long after that, at nine years old, my beloved father passed away. I was devastated. In my childlike mind I wondered if I had somehow caused his death, with the stress of everything we had gone through as a family.

I grew up in an era and culture where, if you appeared functional, it was considered best to not talk about what had happened or your feelings. So we all just 'got on with it'. It wasn't a strategy that was working well for me. Outwardly I was bubbly, happy and gregarious. I had plenty of friends; I did well at school and had boyfriends. So nothing seemed to be amiss, however deep down inside I was incredibly unhappy and insecure.

By the time I was nineteen it all came to a head. I had just broken up with my boyfriend but was still living at his place because I didn't know where to go. I had taken a gap year from university and was waitressing. I didn't know whether to continue at university or find a career. I had wanted to be an actress but I hated the idea of auditions and wondered if I really had the talent to make it. Then all of a sudden, almost inexplicably, I began to feel incredibly hopeless. It was as though my life would never change. I felt that moments of happiness were just a fantasy escape from the reality of depression.

I remember standing at the sink of my boyfriend's grandmother's house with a small handful of her sleeping tablets in my hand and a glass of water. I put the pills in my mouth and stopped for a moment. I considered that what I was doing was a pathetic cry for help and that I didn't really want to kill myself but I also didn't know what else to do. So I swallowed them. My ex-boyfriend came home, realised what I had done and made me throw them up. It was a completely humiliating experience.

After that it was panic stations; understandably the people around me did not know what to do with me. When I look back on it now I realise how frightening this must have been for them. I had suddenly become unpredictable and obviously needed help. So I made the rounds of counsellors. I remember finding someone I liked and telling him my story and even though it was good to talk I didn't really feel like anything was resolved. It was a wonderful first step but it wasn't anywhere near the final one.

Not long after that I was talking to a very perceptive friend of mine. He said to me: "You know Pip, it is like there are two of you. The bubbly surface one and someone deeper, troubled whom I don't have the skills to reach." He suggested I go to see his spiritual teacher.

So off I went. I remember knocking on the door to her home with great trepidation. A strong Greek woman answered and looked at me with large, penetrating eyes. I knew at that moment that something special was going to occur however I was terribly frightened. She invited me in and sat me down. Then the first question she asked me was: "Why don't you just slash your wrists?" I was shocked and angry. How dare she speak to me that way! I burst into tears and confessed "I don't really want to die, I just want to escape the pain", and she said to me: "Good, then we can do something about it."

That began a journey that spanned twenty-two years. I went to her home almost every day except when I was overseas or simply taking a break. I helped raise her children and performed tasks for her such as the washing and housework. She was very particular about these domestic tasks, and I can say housework is definitely not one of my talents! In return she taught me The 8 Principles of Achievement. She also taught me The 7 Principles of Growth and Abundance and The 7 Principles of Transformation and Influence, the last two of which will be the subject of another book.

At first I applied The Principles to healing my soul and then began applying them to my life. It was a slow, intense process. The way I was taught was not structured, it was more like a yogic apprenticeship or learning a spiritual discipline. It was The Principles applied to everyday life, emotion and thought. Often the lessons were highly intuitive and I would only realise much later what I had learnt or what my teacher meant. This was fantastic and challenging for me. It was an ancient way of learning that allowed The Principles to become part of my DNA, the very core of my being. I wanted to share The Principles with others but I realised most people did not have twenty-two years to devote to this learning. Yet I felt they could still gain the most incredible insights from understanding The Principles.

I wanted the information to be more accessible and available. I began looking at other modalities of change. At that point I discovered NLP (Neuro Linguistic Programming) and Transformational Coaching tools. At first I couldn't believe that the techniques were so fast and effective. I was able to get results very quickly. I was very excited and for a while I left behind The Principles. But when I started to coach using NLP and teach it I realised I was getting results with clients which were much deeper and more profound than many of my colleagues. It occurred to me that I was intuitively using The Principles and these were having a massive impact on my client's outcomes and my own success.

I began to consciously use The Principles to fill in areas I felt were missing in the NLP and the Life Coaching techniques I had been taught. The first gap I saw was in clearing grief. I realised many people couldn't overcome grief if they felt there was something unresolved with the person who had passed away. Using The Principles and my own personal experience with grief I created a Grief Clearing Script to overcome this issue.

Within a few months I had already created a series of techniques and scripts aimed particularly at clearing disempowering patterns of behaviour picked up from parents. I called my techniques Matrix Therapies® Coaching. I started teaching these techniques to small groups. Coaches began using my techniques to get incredibly profound results with clients. The techniques could also be used to clear the influence of abusers and other negative people in a person's life. I created techniques for overcoming a lack of self-esteem and self-love. I also applied The Principles to improve techniques of clearing negative emotions and beliefs and to deal with stuck repeated patterns that were resistant to change.

These were all the issues I had faced in my own life and I found combining the structure of Coaching and NLP with the profundity and intuition of The Principles really created something deeper, more powerful and completely original. It was and still is incredibly exciting.

For more than fifteen years I have combined my twenty-two years of understanding The Principles with coaching techniques to provide a suite of personal development tools and courses that people can also use if they want to become a therapeutic and transformational coach. As well as Matrix Therapies® Coaching, the techniques now include Passion and Purpose Coaching™, Masculine and Feminine Coaching™, Achievement Love and Happiness Coaching™, Growth and Abundance Coaching™ and Transformation and Influence Coaching™. These techniques all sit under the banner of a new field I have called Archetypal Coaching® because they use the enduring and archetypal tools of The Principles.

When I studied The Principles there were many names for each principle and sometimes the secrets to achieving each one was not clear or even completely missing. So I have used my expertise and experience to create easily identifiable names for each principle and the exact corresponding secret. This ensures you can use the principle successfully. This is my personal contribution to this work.

My other contribution has been to clarify each principle so it can be more easily applied in your life. So I have created exercises and coaching tools that are totally new and form a complete system of personal transformation and development. This makes using The Principles practical while still maintaining their profundity. As many of the coaching tools I have created are designed for live training or for one-on-one coaching, I have adjusted them to work in written form.

I have also spent many years and countless hours analysing how The Principles work in order and unison. So the way The Principles are presented in this book is very different from the form I originally studied. Over the past fifteen years I have created a huge body of work of which this book is simply an introduction. My aim however has been to make this extraordinary wisdom available to a wider audience in a way that is easy to understand and apply. In my courses and coaching we are able to explore The Principles in greater depth for you personally. The courses can also qualify you as a coach to assist other people's transformation.

Matrix Therapies® Coaching and Archetypal Coaching® based on The Principles have now been used in every state of Australia and spread internationally to Europe, USA, China, Indonesia, New Zealand and most recently Israel.

It has been my privilege to study and use The Principles for over 30 years and now to share these same Principles with you, so that you too can improve every area of your life, be it career, relationships, health or wellbeing. I wish you every joy in learning and happiness in success.

With warmth,

Pip McKay

# OUTLINE OF THE 8 PRINCIPLES OF ACHIEVEMENT, LOVE AND HAPPINESS

In order to achieve what we want in life there are The 8 Principles to follow. If we have an issue or block with one or more of these principles we will not achieve what we want or not be happy with our results. We then feel disappointed and frustrated. When we follow The 8 Principles we achieve success while feeling fulfilled, loving and happy.

Not getting what we want is part of the growth process that keeps us adjusting until we can either achieve our goals or change what we desire into something that makes us happier. However, if we are constantly disappointed this is not conducive to our evolution. Disappointment and frustration are tools that let us know that there is one or more of The 8 Principles of Achievement that are out of balance or not being used effectively. When we work on that area and resolve the issues surrounding it, our life comes into flow and it is easier for us to achieve what really make us happy. The Principles are also designed to work in the order presented below.

The 8 Principles of Achievement are:

1. **The Principle of Energy – The Law of Belief**
   The Secret of Inspiration
   The Power of Enthusiasm
   The Fiery Intelligence
   **Innocent Adventurer Archetype**

2. **The Principle of Concentration – The Law of Attraction**
   The Secret of Focus
   The Power of Transformation

The Transparent Intelligence
   **Magician Archetype**

3. **The Principle of Receptivity – The Law of Acceptance**
   The Secret of Vulnerability
   The Power of Magnetism
   The Uniting Intelligence
   **Oracle Archetype**

4. **The Principle of Creativity – The Law of Abundance**
   The Secret of Imagination
   The Power of Love
   The Luminous Intelligence
   **Creative Nurturer Archetype**

5. **The Principle of Organisation – The Law of Protection**
   The Secret of Insight
   The Power of Power
   The Constituting Intelligence
   **Ruler Archetype**

6. **The Principle of Intuition – The Law of Wisdom**
   The Secret of Listening
   The Power of Knowing
   The Triumphant Intelligence
   **Sage Archetype**

7. **The Principle of Discernment – The Law of Connection**
   The Secret of Self-Love
   The Power of Decisions
   The Disposing Intelligence
   **Lovers Archetype**

8. **The Principle of Results – The Law of Completion**
   The Secret of Action
   The Power of Persistence
   The Influential Intelligence
   **Knight Archetype**

# IMPORTANCE OF THE ORDER OF THE PRINCIPLES

The 8 Principles of Achievement work in the specific order outlined previously and explained below. Sometimes people do not achieve what they want because they skip steps or do them the wrong way around. For instance, many people criticise their work and want to make it perfect before they have given themselves the freedom to be creative. This just causes creative blocks or a rehashing of old, safe ideas. When we create first and then order later we can produce something truly profound. So to achieve what we really want and be happy with the outcome:

1. We need to firstly be inspired, which gives us the energy and enthusiasm to begin.

2. Then we need to concentrate on one thing and focus our time and energy on that one thing.

3. In the next step we need to be open to receive. So many people focus on what they want but they push away the very thing they desire because of hidden fears in the subconscious mind. We need to ensure we are truly willing to receive what we want. This takes a form of vulnerability because we are admitting to what we really want and then magnetising to us the people and resources that will help us make it happen.

4. Now it is time to imagine clearly what we desire and put the time and effort into creating it. It is important to fall in love with what you want so you are willing to do what it takes to nurture it into being. Think about what you would be willing to do for your child. This same level of commitment is needed to create what you truly desire.

5. Next it is important to have keen insight into what you have created and to provide the structures and systems that will support its growth. This requires organisation and the power to protect what you have created from outside influences that may distract you or even rubbish your ideas.

6. Following this you need to let your creation rest a little, have some time out so you can listen to your intuition and see if anything more is needed. This gives you much wisdom and profundity.

7. Then it is important to become aware of what to keep and what to trim. In a book or course or anything you create there are sections you may like but are irrelevant to the topic. You need to have enough self-love and confidence to cut those things away so that others can easily understand what you have created. You also need to let go of others' judgments so you can express yourself clearly. This calls for the ability to discern and to make decisions.

8. Finally, take action and persist in that action until you obtain results. This gives you the momentum to promote what you have created so that others can see it, buy it and tell others about it, particularly if it is a product or service. If you want a relationship the same principle applies; you need to let others know what you want so they know you are available.

These are The 8 Principles of Achievement and proper application of these Principles will ensure success.

# WHERE DO THE 8 PRINCIPLES COME FROM?

The 8 Principles of Achievement are actually a part of *The 22 Principles of Success*. As well as these first 8 Principles there are also The 7 Principles of Growth and Abundance and The 7 Principles of Transformation and Influence. If we cannot grow we will not maintain what we have achieved and our results will eventually stagnate and decay. This is why The 7 Principles of Growth and Abundance are essential to maintaining success. We also need to be able to transform when necessary so we can adapt to new circumstances and not be left behind. This is where The 7 Principles of Transformation and Influence are also essential for success. In order to have true success we need to be able to achieve, then grow and finally transform. Together these total *The 22 Principles of Success*.

What is clear however is that the first step is to achieve because you have nothing to grow or transform if you have not first achieved. For instance, in business, you first have to create the business before you can grow it and then later transform it.

The true origin of the *The 22 Principles of Success* is probably lost in the mist of time, however some believe the following explanation, although no one can currently attest to its accuracy. I relay it purely for the sake of interest. The truth of this explanation, or lack thereof, in no way affects the authenticity, profundity and power of The Principles. You can test their power by applying them in your everyday life and seeing the incredible results.

Most people have heard of the burning of the Library of Alexandria in 48BC by Julius Caesar, where it is estimated that between 40,000 and 400,000 scrolls were lost. What most people don't know is that the libraries of Egypt had a long history of being burnt and knowledge lost.

The story goes that during this time it was decided to reduce all the information down to 22 Principles, which summed up successful human consciousness. It was thought that if these 22 Principles were known and fully understood people could discover all the information that ever was, is, and will be. In this way the thinking that led to the knowledge could be preserved even if the knowledge itself was lost.

It is important to remember what an incredible centre of learning Egypt was in ancient times. Pythagoras spent many years in Egypt as of course did Alexander the Great. There was a great interaction between Greece and Egypt, and Alexandria was re-founded as a Hellenistic city. The Egyptian mystery schools and learning had a great impact on the Greek philosophers, such as Plato and Aristotle.

Egypt was a melting pot of knowledge which resulted from trade with diverse cultures, such as India, Africa, China, Persia, Arabia and Israel, that mixed with its own advanced and ancient wisdom. As a result, The 22 Principles gathered the most profound knowledge from all the great spiritual, cultural and philosophical teachings.

At some point, perhaps in Fez, Morocco, pictures were made of The 22 Principles creating Archetypal images that allowed for ease of communication of ideas between different cultures and schools of thought.

With the continual wars and destruction of knowledge it became important to spread The Principles as far as possible so that they would not be lost. Their power however was kept a mystery. The best way to keep many secrets hidden is right under people's noses. So The 22 Principles were used as the subject of art, music, poetry and literature using Archetypal images and themes. Very few people had the keys to unlock their power because these keys were considered closely guarded secrets.

Seekers of knowledge could be initiated into the wisdom and then sworn to secrecy. The resulting Mystery Schools then spread through out Egypt, India, Africa, China, Greece and Jerusalem and later Europe, the United Kingdom and finally in more recent times ending up in the United Sates and Asia Pacific. It is clear that at seminal points in history key people have gained this wisdom and it has led to a bubbling up of creativity, knowledge, power and riches depending on the nature and interests of the person using The 22 Principles and what success meant to them.

During the Dark Ages, when the knights went to Jerusalem, they brought back knowledge that had a massive impact on European civilization. Before that Europe was barbaric and basic; afterwards there was a flowering of art and culture. This knowledge took southern France, in particular, out of the Dark Ages and ushered in the Middle Ages. As a result southern France had a Renaissance of ideas that pre-dated other areas of Europe. The Knights Templar were privy to this information, and this, along with other treasures, created immense power for them. They were also able to structure, organise and create with a clarity that had previously been unimaginable.

When this information was lost during the Cathar Crusade and the suppression of the Knights Templar there was a downturn in knowledge and progress until the Renaissance. At that time the great families such as the Viscontis, Sforzas and Medicis went on a quest for secret knowledge. The Medicis in particular gathered wisdom from Ancient Greece, as well as what was brought back from the Holy Land and hidden in monasteries. The dissemination of this knowledge led to a Golden Age of creativity and genius, with people like Brunelleschi, Michelangelo, Botticelli, Leonardo da Vinci and Rafael flourishing under the patronage of the Medicis.

Elizabeth the First had access to this ancient knowledge, as did William Shakespeare and Francis Bacon, and this ushered in the Golden Age of Art, Science and Literature in England. Later, the Age of Enlightenment was also influenced by this knowledge. In the 19th Century artistic figures such as Dante Gabriel Rossetti, who formed The Secret Brotherhood of the Pre-Raphaelite Movement, were initiates into these mysteries. Their art is still some of the most popular today. Even people who don't know anything about art are still attracted to these paintings. They continue to buy the prints due to the impact of the symbolic meanings hidden within them, which add intrigue to their incredible beauty.

With all our modern innovation and technology people feel a kind of soullessness and disconnection. They yearn for deeper meaning and understanding, and this is where the need for The 22 Principles is re-emerging. The problem in our modern world is that most people do not have the time to be immersed in this wisdom and assimilate it. When small elements are leaked into the public without context it is often done so simplistically as to become ineffective. For example, the Law of Attraction is one of The 22 Principles and this is why the book based on it became such a massive phenomenon. However without the other 21 Principles to support it, people felt disappointed and disillusioned by the almost wishful thinking it engendered. Instead we want to use The Principles to first focus on what we want and then take step by step action towards it. This includes persisting when we face obstacles along the way until we achieve the result we want.

Instead, The 22 Principles form an art and science of thinking, feeling and behaving that leads not only to success but also engenders a profound sense of being. These principles are inside all of us and we access them intuitively every day. However, without a full knowledge of The Principles, success and happiness become a hit and miss affair. When The 22 Principles are applied effectively they become the keys to gaining that elusive Holy Grail of achievement, love and happiness.

More recently in the United States of America, the Principles influenced the American Constitution. Later during the the Great Depression the Principles informed the seminal book *Think and Grow Rich*, which assisted those who had nothing to create wealth through the power of their mind.

**SECTION 1**

# The 8 Principles of Achievement, Love and Happiness

EXPLANATION OF EACH PRINCIPLE
AND PRACTICAL EXERCISES
FOR APPLICATION

# THE PRINCIPLE OF Energy

**CHAPTER 1**

# THE PRINCIPLE OF ENERGY

Many people feel tired and long to have more energy, they look at children and sigh: "Oh, I wish I had their energy." They believe that getting older means less vitality.

Instead the real problem is that they do not understand the Principle of Energy. Of course it is important to get enough sleep and nutrition but it is possible to get eight hours sleep and eat well and still lack drive. It is also possible to have more energy as you get older than you did as a teenager.

### The Secret to Energy is Inspiration

The reason children look like they have more energy is because people observe them when they are having fun or doing something they like. Observe a child having to do something they don't want to do and you will see a child with no energy.

As William Shakespeare famously said:

> "Love goes toward love, as schoolboys from their books,
> but love from love, toward school with heavy looks."

Think about it, have you ever felt very tired and then someone suggests a great idea for something to do and you find yourself re-energised?

Have you ever felt bored at work and then out of the blue there is a new, exciting project and you find yourself re-inspired and energised?

Have you ever been falling asleep listening to a speaker when suddenly they say something that inspires your interest and immediately your eyes are wide open?

Have you ever come up with an idea of something you really want to do or a place you want to travel to and immediately you feel enthused and could stay up all night planning it?

The common denominator in all these situations is inspiration. You can be exhausted and then instantly be inspired and have a huge boost of energy.

For a moment remember someone who is bored with what they do or with life in general – they are always lacking in motivation and energy. In fact, to be around someone like this is draining. It is as though they are attempting to draw the energy they are missing from you.

Now think about someone you know, have seen or read about, who is inspired and passionate. They are the type of people you want to hang around with. They are magnetic, they draw you in with their enthusiasm and vision. They are the leaders people want to follow.

Their charisma has nothing to do with how they look, their colour, class or creed…their energy comes from their inspiration and their ability to communicate that inspiration to you with enthusiasm.

## The Innocent Adventurer

There are some people who embody the Principle of Energy. It is as if energy and inspiration oozes out of them. We call these people Innocent Adventurers. They make this principle seem easy and are an inspiration to others to enjoy life more and have fun.

Think of Richard Branson, the Dalai Lama, Ellen DeGeneres or Whoopi Goldberg; these are all people who are inspired and enthusiastic and their energy is contagious. They are all examples of Innocent Adventurers. They are not afraid of the new or trying something outlandish. They laugh and have a child-like quality that draws people in and keeps them interested with their quirky sense of humour and unpredictable style.

If you want more energy, do something new, different or unexpected. Feel the rush of adrenaline that makes you feel alive and then watch people light up as you tell them about it. You might like to pick one of the people above or think of someone you know who is an Innocent

Adventurer and ask yourself something like: "What would Richard Branson do in this situation to make it more fun and motivational?"

## Archetypal Innocent Adventurer

All cultures have examples of the Innocent Adventurer Archetype. They inspire people to think outside the box and follow their impulses, to have fun or be mischievous. Thinking differently inspires creativity and problem solving but it also allows us to laugh at ourselves and not take ourselves too seriously.

One of my favourite examples of this is Hanuman in the Ramayana stories from India. He is half-human and half-monkey, and in his youth used to play tricks on the Yogis who were meditating to distract them. He also found fun by entertaining his friends and providing unexpected food for poor fishermen and farmers. As he grows and matures he is less disruptive but he never loses his sense of humour. This allows him to get out of trouble and see things differently to other people. It is this ability that enables him to rescue the princess Sita and return her to Rama.

> ### My Experience
>
> When I was 19 I caught glandular fever and it led to bouts of chronic fatigue throughout my life. Even though my body was often exhausted and needed extra rest and nutrition I was still able to run my business successfully because I was inspired and had fun. If I repeated teaching a course too many times and was bored I could feel the chronic fatigue catching up with me, but the moment I had a new and exciting idea the fatigue left me.
>
> Whenever I taught something I loved people would always comment on how much energy I had, but it was really the inspiration that was sustaining and firing me up. After the course finished and the inspiration was momentarily gone, I would need to rest and recover however my energy was always there for me when I needed it. All I had to do was ensure I was inspired. Eventually I found solutions that allowed my body to overcome the chronic fatigue, but if I had not known the Principle of Energy I would not have been able to sustain my business and creativity.

##  Your Turn

Remember a time when you felt inspired, a specific time, and remember how much energy you had at that moment. Now think about what was causing you to feel inspired. Was it creativity, something new, the thought of an adventure or maybe a connection with someone you liked. Take a moment and write a list of five words that make you feel inspired.

At times when you are lacking in energy look at your words and see if they are present in your current situation. It is likely they are not. Now take each word and see how you can apply that word to change your current situation. Perhaps one of the words is freedom. Brainstorm ways you can feel more free in your current situation. Maybe it is by having a more flexible start time or simply not taking work or business home. You will be surprised how much your productivity goes up in the day if you don't allow yourself to work at night.

## An Example of this Exercise

My words of inspiration are magic, freedom, adventure, creativity and passion. If I am tired I look at these words and ask myself: "Is there any magic, freedom, adventure, creativity and passion in what I am currently doing?"

If I feel uninspired these things are usually missing. Then I ask myself how can I make this situation more magical, free, adventurous, creative and passionate for others and myself.

A while ago, I found myself lacking in energy and did this exercise. The upshot was I decided to take a group of people to southern France in Search of the Holy Grail and what it really means as a metaphor for life. I immediately felt re-inspired and re-energised. This idea fulfilled all my inspiration ideals. Travelling always makes me feel free and a quest for the Holy Grail is the ultimate magical adventure. I could also create a new course and I am passionate about medieval stories and all things French.

Previously, travel adventures were separate from my work but by doing this exercise I could combine this area of inspiration with my business. The course sold very quickly and with little effort and I could travel as a tax deduction, what a bonus!

## The Principle of Energy applied to gaining Success, Love and Happiness

Many people seriously search for happiness, turning themselves inside out in its pursuit. I certainly believe unresolved issues from the past have a huge effect on how happy we feel and it is important to receive some coaching to clear them. Sometimes however we can get too bogged down in our problems and forget to have fun.

After all, it is not easy to be happy if you are not inspired by your career, relationships or lifestyle. Thinking about what you feel passionate about and incorporating these into your life is a key to happiness. Laughing and having energy is of course going to contribute to feelings of joy.

I had a client once who came to me and said: "I only have one goal and that is to be happy and I just don't feel happy at all." The first thing I asked him to do was to brainstorm all the things that made him feel happy. We ended up listing over twenty activities that he felt inspired by or were simply fun to do. We whittled this down to his top five activities.

Then we looked at a snapshot of a typical week of his life. There was not a single thing in his week that made him feel happy or inspired. None of his top-five happiness activities were present. He really disliked his job, which took up about sixty hours of his week. He often took work home because he considered himself to be inefficient at work. This then took up much of his Saturday as he tried to catch up. By the time Sunday came along he felt tired and despondent and found himself veg'ing out in front of the TV. He considered this a huge waste of time but he didn't have the energy to do anything else. Much of the rest of his time was taken up by domestic duties, which he found incredibly boring. Sounds like a recipe for depression – he literally was not doing a single thing in his life that he wanted to do.

The top three things he loved to do and found inspiring were going to the gym, being outdoors in nature and socialising. The first thing we did was ban him from taking work home on Saturdays. He had to do his work at work or not get it done. This meant his Saturdays were now free. He then had time to go to the gym, go outdoors and socialise. By Sunday he didn't feel like veg'ing out in front of the TV and this gave him another whole day to do the things he loved.

Not surprisingly he found it easier to get his work done in the time allocated at the office because he was highly motivated and this greatly increased his productivity. He could then leave work at a reasonable time and go for a walk, go to the gym or catch up with friends.

We then started to look at a career option that incorporated more of what he loved to do. Of course becoming a personal trainer came to mind because it incorporated going to the gym, being outdoors and socialising. It seems obvious, doesn't it? But when people are uninspired it is as if they have blinkers on and can't see solutions that are obvious to others. This is because they feel trapped in a cycle of doing what they have to do instead of seeing possibilities of how they could make money from what they love to do.

He made his transition responsibly and kept his job while he gained his personal training qualifications. His inspiration gave him the energy to study and work at the same time. He also found his work much more enjoyable because he knew it was funding his new career and he was being more productive and proactive.

During his coaching we also cleared negative patterns and attitudes he had picked up from his parents to make his transition easier. His father had done a job he found boring his whole life because he thought it was the only way he could support his family. His mother gave up a career she loved to look after the children and never returned.

So you can see he had simply repeated the negative pattern passed on from his parents. By receiving coaching in this area he was able to break free from this generational influence and step into his own passion and purpose, and this gave him energy and happiness.

By the time he finished his coaching most of his week involved doing things he loved, and he felt much, much happier. He even employed a cleaner to get rid of some of those boring domestic duties. It wasn't long before he was working as a personal trainer, and because he was very passionate about it people loved him. His inspiration energised his clients and they raved about him to others. This of course meant he had a steady stream of clients allowing him to be successful at this new career.

I caught up with this client a number of years later and not only was he still very happy doing what he was doing but he had also found his love partner through his work. He said that previously he had always thought settling down would make him feel trapped, but after coaching he could see ways of doing things differently from his parents. He now wanted to become a loving husband and an inspiring dad.

# THE PRINCIPLE OF Concentration

**CHAPTER 2**

# THE PRINCIPLE OF CONCENTRATION

This Principle is the same as the Law of Attraction and, as I am sure you are aware, was the subject of the movie, *The Secret*. This is a real and important principle but it does not work in isolation. It needs to work with the other 7 Principles of Achievement in order to be effective. It is the all-important second step after energy. After all, if you don't know what you want, you can't concentrate on it and that means it is not easy to attract into your life. When you know what you want you can focus your energy, make decisions, organise your time and take action towards your goal.

## The Secret to Concentration is Focus

One of the traits that make successful people achieve so much is their ability to focus on what they want and cut away distractions. The ability to focus and concentrate does create a kind of magical attraction. When you know what you want you concentrate your efforts, and other people want to help you achieve your vision.

Your Reticular Activating System, or RAS for short, is a part of the brain that allows you to ignore unimportant details in your environment and take notice of what is important to you, wanted or needed. This is an extremely important function of the brain. If you think of all the millions of pieces of information that are bombarding your nervous system every day, you would literally go crazy if you could not filter the dross out.

When you decide you want a new car or pet it is your RAS that suddenly makes you notice them everywhere. Suddenly it is as if the world is filled with them.

If you do not decide what you want the RAS cannot help you see it or find it in your environment. In fact if you do not set your own goals and train your RAS, it will simply help you repeat your parental programming. In other words it will help you get what someone else wanted instead of what you want.

For instance, if your Dad or Mum failed in business and they then told you it is better to get a secure job. Your RAS would show you examples of people who have failed in business. It would then filter out successful businesses and business opportunities. Even if you do notice successful business people you may come to the conclusion that it is OK for them but not for you. This attitude may stop you from gaining the necessary skills and educating yourself on how to have a successful business. Then if you have a moment of inspiration about business you may lack the persistence and concentration to overcome the usual obstacles to make the business work because the negative belief is working against you at every turn.

There are two ways to train the RAS; the first is to know and focus on what you want and then continue to concentrate on gaining the necessary skills and taking the necessary action until you achieve the result you are looking for. The other is to clear away negative programming, emotions and beliefs that may be holding you back.

Personally, I find an approach that does both is the fastest and most effective way to get what you want. When you can focus your RAS on what you want and are not influenced by old programming, or naysayers, magical transformations happen and people are amazed by the results you can gain. Although these changes may seem magical to others, you will know that getting what you wanted took focus, attention and commitment.

Of course, some things you want may be supported by your parental programming. Your parents may have had a loving and stable relationship. Then when you decide you want to have that commitment your RAS is already supporting that decision and it becomes easy to make that a focus in your life. However, this still depends on knowing what you want.

As Jim Rohn, famous USA motivational speaker once said: "If you know what you want and want it bad enough you will find a way to get it."

## The Magician

There are some people who embody the Principle of Concentration. It is as if their ability to focus and achieve is magical. They are able to create things out of their imagination that others would find impossible or improbable. We call these people Magicians.

Think of people like Walt Disney, JK Rowling, Steven Frayne aka Dynamo Magician Impossible, or Stephen Hawkins.

These are all people who made the impossible possible. Before Mickey Mouse, imagine someone saying they were going to become rich on the back of a cute moving drawing of a mouse. Remember before Mickey Mouse this kind of animation didn't exist. Walt Disney built his entire empire on making magic happen but without his incredible focus and concentrated effort he could not have made his vision a reality.

In order to attract more of what you want in your life then decide on what it is you want and focus all your attention, energy and commitment to getting it. If you experience the inevitable setbacks, use them to learn more effective ways of obtaining what you want and doubling your focus and commitment. Then see how the world of possibilities opens up for you and you begin to attract situations and people who assist you.

You may like to select one of the people above or think of someone you know who is a Magician and study their lives. Notice that they had their fair share of failures. Discover what strategies and beliefs they had that allowed them to overcome their problems, create resilience and continue to focus on their goals. Then make a commitment to do the same.

## Archetypal Magician

All cultures have examples of the Magician Archetype. They show people that magic is the result of developing skills and maintaining focus. What is magic to the observer is actually the result of the ability to concentrate on developing a craft.

My favourite example of this is the shaman of many traditional cultures. The magical healing that often occurs comes from a specialised apprenticeship and study of medicinal herbs, psychology and spiritual truths.

> ## My Experience
>
> Years ago when I was teaching Neuro Linguistic Programming (NLP), a particularly perceptive student said to me: "When I watch you do demonstrations, I can see you are using the techniques but I feel like there is something else going on and I don't know what it is. Something that is intuitive. What is that? I would like to learn that, it's magical."
>
> It was at that point I decided it was time to teach The Principles. I realised I had spent so much time studying and focusing on The Principles that they informed everything I did. Even though I was using NLP and Coaching techniques the quality of my insights was giving me a massive advantage that my students didn't have.
>
> It looked magical because my students didn't have the formula and strategies of developing advanced levels of consciousness, which The Principles provide. I began teaching The Principles to a small group of invitation-only students. When I thought about who to invite that observant student was at the top of my list. It has been years now since she learnt those tools and we are still in contact. To this day she often says to me: "I am so glad I learnt The Principles. I use them every day and don't know where I would be without them. They have been so incredible for me both personally and professionally."

 **Your Turn**

Take a moment to close your eyes, take a few breaths and get a sense of something you want to achieve which is really important to you. Make this goal crystal clear in your mind. Get a picture, sound and feeling of exactly what it will be like when you achieve this goal. Fill in the details of what it will look, sound and feel like when this goal is a reality for you.

Now list all the reasons why you want this goal and why these results are important to you. List all the benefits this goal will bring you in the future and the highest purpose of this goal.

Now look at what you need to learn and do in order to achieve this goal. Think about what obstacles may present themselves and what strategies or resources you will call upon to overcome these possible obstacles. Write all of these down and prioritise what you need to learn or do first. Break these steps into baby steps that you can do every day.

Make a commitment to yourself that you will consistently do whatever it takes in order to achieve your goal. Even if you have other pressing tasks, make sure you take baby steps every day. Focus on your goal and concentrate on completing each step towards the final outcome.

In the end time passes – but will time passing result in you obtaining the things you want or will it just pass you by?

## An Example of this Exercise

Years ago I lived in an inner western suburb of Sydney. Every day I would catch a train further west to work. At the train station I would wish I was going in the opposite direction towards Manly and the beach.

At the time this desire was simply wishful thinking. I took no proactive steps towards my goal. One day I realised that wishful thinking was never going to bring me my goal and I began doing the exercise outlined above.

My baby steps were to first write down and picture my ideal home. Then I simply went to Manly and looked at property. I had no idea what property cost in Manly and couldn't set a financial goal without that knowledge.

I looked at a lot of properties in my price range that I didn't like. One day I was with my mum on yet another frustrating property search when on a whim I saw a particular ad for an apartment I simply couldn't afford. My intuition however clearly said; "Stop the car I am going to look at this one". My mum was so tired from all our previous searching she decided to wait in the car.

I walked into the apartment and immediately knew it was my future home. It had everything I wanted. It took up the whole floor and had light coming in on all sides. It was on a hill so at the front it had a view and at the back it had a garden. This was virtually unheard of in Manly and something I really wanted for my menagerie of animals. It was also an art deco building with high ceilings. When I looked up at the fantastic ceiling roses I saw that they had the motif of two Griffins holding the Holy Grail, wow!

I decided then and there I would do whatever it took to own that apartment. Previously, I had wanted to hold on to my first property and borrow money to buy my dream home but it would have taken me years to save up that money at that time. The solution was simple; I had to let go of that old belief that was holding me back and sell my first home. That gave me the money I needed to buy my dream home and I have lived there happily ever since. Having a clear goal, taking steps towards it and doing whatever it takes to achieve it really is a form of magic.

## The Principle of Concentration applied to gaining Success, Love and Happiness

I once had a client who came to me for mentoring in order to create a successful coaching business. She was very into the Law of Attraction but was completely bewildered by it. In her first session with me she said: "I don't know what happened. I totally focused on what I wanted and visualised it clearly. Then I sent out an email to the people on my email address book saying I had set up a coaching business. I clearly stated I was offering a free one-hour session but only one person replied. I emailed back and forth with her to make an appointment and then she didn't turn up."

This client obviously had a mistaken belief about how much work it took to build up loyal clientele. She had read about the Law of Attraction and then had unrealistic expectations of what was needed to gain people's interest. I knew from my own experience that simply sending out a single email was never going to be enough for her to have the results she was looking for.

First she needed to build up a database in an automated system, then she needed to give them valuable information so they were interested in what she did and trusted her. Then finally she needed to give them her offer with clear benefits as to why they should take it up. It was going to take a great deal more concentrated effort, work and skill than she had applied so far.

In the end I started by asking her how she had come to see me. She went through quite a detailed story as to how a friend had seen me speak at a breakfast meeting and had then sent her a link to my website. She had then watched my videos and read a blog. She signed up to a newsletter and been invited to a webinar. After the webinar she decided to call me.

It didn't take long for the penny to drop. Setting up a successful coaching business was going to take a lot more than simply visualising and sending an email. In the end she concentrated on getting a speaking gig and her first clients were inspired to come to her because she gave a great speech.

In terms of love she already had a good relationship. Working for herself as a coach gave her much more flexibility than her corporate career had done. This meant she could go on more holidays and spend more time with her partner. This really gave both her love life and her happiness a much needed boost.

The wonderful thing about the Principle of Concentration is that it allows you to know what tasks you should focus on and what to let go. You should only let go of tasks that take you away from focusing on your outcome. Most people delegate the tasks they don't like to do and this can be a mistake. The first tasks that should be delegated are the tasks that support you achieving your outcome but are not essential to you producing a result.

For instance, if you own a small business YOU are the best sales person for your product or service. In the early stages you should not be delegating sales because it is essential to the success of your business. Book-keeping however is a good task to delegate because, even though it is incredibly important to the ongoing functioning of your business, it is not essential to achieving initial success. If right now your books are a mess you may at tax time need to focus on bringing them up to speed but then, as soon as you can, you need a competent book-keeper. They can then take over the figures and you can factor in monthly meetings so you understand them..

I see too many small business owners spending their precious day-to-day time on their books and ignoring sales because they feel more comfortable crunching numbers than getting out into the public arena. Without any money coming in there are no numbers to crunch! When you have brought money in then you have the money to find a good book-keeper.

As your business progresses and you have systematised the successful sales process you can begin to bring in sales people but until then all the delegation should be on support staff. They are also cheaper to hire. This allows you to let go of administration and focus your time and attention on bringing in more money and making sure there is a superior level of service. Then word of mouth becomes a powerful sales tool.

# THE PRINCIPLE OF Receptivity

**CHAPTER 3**

# THE PRINCIPLE OF RECEPTIVITY

Many people are able to attract what they want but they then push it away or sabotage it because they do not know how to receive. The ability to receive is one of the hidden Principles of Achievement and many people have major problems with this concept. Often people can't even receive a compliment graciously and then wonder why they don't obtain and retain the things they want. One of the reasons people have such issues with receptivity is because of the secret attached to it.

## The Secret to Receptivity is Vulnerability

Think about it for a moment. When you give a gift, who is in control of what the gift is? That's right – you are. Who is in control of when the gift is given? Yep, you guessed it – you are. Who is in control of the intention behind the gift? Yes, right again – you are. So basically when you give a gift or even a compliment you are the one who is in control.

But when you receive a gift…you are not in control of what the gift is, when it is given to you, or what the intention behind the gift is. This makes you vulnerable because as the receiver you do not have control.

The only thing you are in control of is your reaction. So as a result a lot of people don't react very well. They say things like: "You shouldn't have!" or "You shouldn't be spending your money on me like that."

This basically pushes the gift away and makes the receiver feel more in control. They have not actually received the gift, nor have they taken the intention of the gift into themselves. This makes people feel less obligated to the giver, they don't have to worry about what the giver expects in return. This is not however a particularly useful message to be giving to others if you want to receive success, love and happiness into your life. It suggests you are not worthy of receiving, that it is not safe to receive and that you cannot trust other people's intentions. After all why shouldn't the person give you a gift?

If a person has high self-esteem they don't mind being vulnerable because they don't believe that exposing themselves will reveal anything negative or make them unsafe. They therefore do not have a need to be constantly in control. They trust that other people give for the joy of giving. If the person's intention is not savory they don't feel obliged because, even though they have received, they have not made any unconscious contracts. The contract they have made is that the pleasure of giving is all the giver should expect and if they expect anything else then this is none of the receiver's business.

Someone with high self esteem can accept gifts and compliments graciously because they feel worthy of receiving, worthy enough to have taken space in the giver's thoughts and actions. They also believe that in exchange the giver deserves their gratitude. This attitude also makes it so much easier to receive success, money and recognition because these things are given to you by others even if it is in exchange for work you have completed. In the end you cannot be successful in anything unless someone gives you money or recognition in exchange for what you do. So it is good to practice becoming accomplished at this by receiving gifts and compliments well. The message you give your subconscious mind is that you don't have to exhaust yourself to gain money, attention or love because you are in the flow of receiving and it comes naturally to you.

## The Oracle

There are some people who embody the Principle of Receptivity. It is as if their ability to be vulnerable and grateful magnetises people and things to them. Sometimes they do not seem to be doing very much to receive; they can seem mysterious and a little dark but their vulnerability is in fact a tremendous and rare quality.

Think of people like Angelina Jolie, Johnny Depp, Jim Morrison or Elizabeth Taylor. These people all embody a mysterious charisma that draws you in. In her early years Angelina Jolie was very dark and plagued by depression. As she grew and matured she was able to use her fame to make people aware of what she calls "Hidden Emergences". In this way she was able to shine the light of awareness on the darkest aspects of human suffering and bring some relief. Without her ability to receive fame and fortune she would not be able to assist others in this way. Even in her most troubled moments she has been able to use her fame and fortune to assist others.

## Archetypal Oracles

All cultures have examples of the Oracle Archetype. They revealed what was hidden and allowed deeper contemplation. My favourite Archetypal Oracle was Pythia the Delphic Oracle in Greece. She simply sat on her mountain top, probably breathing in some psychedelic fumes, and people came to her even though her advice was incredibly cryptic and almost impossible to decipher. She was magnetic and her fame still survives today – people love a mystery!

> ### My Experience
>
> Once when I was in Hawaii attending a course, I met a woman who had been one of Elizabeth Taylor's make-up artists. I asked her what Elizabeth Taylor was like and she said: "Oh, she was lovely and I can totally understand why she was bought all those jewels." Now I love jewellery so I was most intrigued to find out what she meant. She told me she noticed Elizabeth did not have the best make-up brushes, so she went out and bought the best brushes and gave them to her as a gift. She said Elizabeth was so grateful and made her feel so special for buying the gift that she wanted to go straight out and buy her something else!
>
> The makeup artist said: "If Richard Burton felt half as good as I did buying Elizabeth these jewels he would certainly spend whatever he had to get her something else, bigger and better than last time. That woman certainly knew how to receive!"
>
> She then told me something even more interesting. On the set was a woman who was selling the most exquisite semi-precious jewellery. The woman asked my friend which piece she liked the best. My friend looked

over the table and saw a piece she loved but, because she thought she wouldn't be able to afford it, she pointed to something smaller that she liked a lot less.

At the end of the shoot Elizabeth Taylor bought all the pieces that people said they liked and gave it to them as a gift. You see Elizabeth had asked the jeweller to make a note of what pieces people loved so she knew what to give them. So my friend received a gift she didn't like all that much when she could have received something that she adored.

She said it was one of the greatest lessons of her life: "I realised that if I couldn't even admit to what I really wanted how was I ever going to receive it?"

From then on she made a point of acknowledging to herself and others what she loved, no matter how vulnerable it made her feel. She let go of worrying about being disappointed or people judging her for wanting too much. Better to be disappointed going for what she wanted than finding out later she could have had it if she had just admitted it to others. Even if she couldn't get what she wanted at least people knew what she liked and what was important to her. She also made a vow that she would always receive gifts and compliments like Elizabeth Taylor. When I heard that story I decided to do the same!

## Your Turn

This is your chance to practice receiving and increase your self-esteem. It is interesting that in our culture there is sometimes a misconception of self-love. Some people see self-love as selfish or 'up yourself', but in fact self-love is the most loving thing you can give to other people. When you love yourself others can share love with you instead of compensating for a lack of love within you. You are more fun to be around and less reactive or needy.

So start by seeing yourself the way someone who loves you sees you.

Begin by simply saying to yourself: "I am beautiful." See yourself as the miracle of creation that you truly are. Focus on your best feature and say the sentence again. Then accept your own compliment by saying: "Thank you – that's lovely, I really appreciate that."

Accepting your own compliments may feel a bit weird to begin with but as you practice this exercise it makes it much easier to accept other people's compliments.

You may find it easier to start with a statement like; "I deserve to be happy". Then accept the statement by saying, "thank you, yes I believe I deserve to be happy".

Repeat the same process with statements such as: "I deserve to be wealthy" and "I deserve to be loved, in and of myself."

Test how you are progressing with these statements. Do any of them make you cringe or can you honestly nd say these statements because they are true? Keep repeating the process until you feel comfortable with the statements and can accept them simply and graciously.

Also, be aware of your thoughts about other people who you consider beautiful, happy, in love and/or wealthy. Check to make sure you are not internally critical or jealous of these people. Blessing other people's gifts and accomplishments are all indicators of how easily you can receive and accept these qualities into your life.

If you are critical of others for these things you will push what *you* want away because the subconscious mind doesn't want someone criticising you in a similar way. When you bless others for what they have your subconscious mind is far more likely to want to bring those things to you, so you can share in those blessings.

## An Example of this Exercise

For many years I did not feel beautiful. I felt if I criticised how I looked I could somehow protect myself from other people's judgments. I felt if I thought I was attractive and others didn't, this would somehow be humiliating.

At a deeper level not only did I fear rejection but I also felt awful rejecting people I didn't want to be with. As a result I preferred to just give the whole dating thing a miss and firmly placed relationships into the 'too hard basket'.

When I decided I wanted to have a long-term partner I knew feeling unattractive and fear of rejection was something I needed to overcome, because it affected my confidence in dating.

So I started doing the exercise above. When I first started with: 'You are beautiful" and then said: "Thank you, that's lovely", I just felt silly. It seemed obvious to me I was not beautiful and saying I was just seemed ridiculous. I decided to do some coaching on this issue – I really wanted to clear the blocks that stopped me having the relationship and love I desired.

The belief I had was, "I am not beautiful". My coach used Byron Katie's *The Work* to challenge this belief. It comprises four questions. The first is: "Is that true?" Whatever the answer the next question is: "Can you absolutely know that it is true?" With this question there is just a 'yes' or 'no' answer. There is no 'sometimes yes' and 'sometimes no' so you must fully contemplate the question.

If there is any exception then the statement cannot be absolutely true.

I knew there were people who considered me beautiful; my mother for one. My father as well, if he were alive, I am sure would think me beautiful. There were friends, ex-boyfriends and children who I knew considered me beautiful. So that meant the statement could not be true!

Hmmm, that put a spanner in the works! The next question was "How do you react, what happens when you believe that thought?" Well it was obvious to me that when I believed the thought that I was not beautiful I had a whole lot of feelings and behaviours that were preventing me from finding my love partner. I noticed that when I found someone attractive I would not look them in the eye. I tended to look down and not smile. I was actually giving the person I liked the impression I did not like them. That certainly was not very useful dating behaviour!

The final question was: "Who would you be without that thought?" Well for me without that thought I would be someone who would be happy, smile, flirt, be confident and make meaningful eye contact. It was clear to me that without that thought I would be someone who could attract my life partner.

The next step is to make the 'turnaround' where you find three genuine examples of how the opposite is true; so for me it was finding examples of how I was beautiful.

I could finally admit that I have absolutely beautiful skin.

I have gorgeous hair.

And most importantly of all, when I feel passionate and inspired, I light up like a Christmas tree, and that is beautiful and compelling.

So now I can easily say: "I am beautiful" and believe it!

That was a huge step forward for me. Not long after that and some other coaching, I found my wonderful life partner and our relationship is an inspiration to all who know us.

Funnily enough my partner often says to me; "You are so beautiful", in his wonderful Irish accent and I say to him: "Thank you, Bunny Rabbit!"

## The Principle of Receptivity applied to gaining Success, Love and Happiness

I had a client who was a very beautiful woman who ran a personal training and coaching business. She originally came to me as a client and then participated in my courses and became a life-coach and trainer. In the initial coaching sessions we were able to assist her to clear some major health and personal issues and she had outstanding results. Then she wanted to work on some of the problems she was having with her staff in her business.

You see, she was an incredibly generous and giving person and this was causing problems in her business. When she employed people she ended up coaching them and making allowances for them. This resulted in her staff costing her more money, time and energy than they were bringing in to the business. It was very draining for her energetically and financially. She even needed to sustain her business by renting out her own home.

The issue was quite complex in structure because as a child she had been encouraged to look after her dysfunctional mother and brother and she had an absent father. She felt her role in the family was to nurture others and this was how she gained significance.

We did a lot of work on clearing the family dynamic and this loosened the issue but didn't completely resolve it. Then in one process, where we were using The Principle of Receptivity, she came to the realisation that her over-giving and self-sacrifice for others was the only way she felt lovable. She felt no one would love her if she was receiving.

Now this conclusion may seem obvious to an outsider but from my experience the most profound changes do not come from a coach telling a client what the problem is. Rather they come from the client having an 'ah ha' moment where they gain a deep emotional realisation of the problem and its resolution.

Through the use of this Principle she was able to learn to stop over-giving and controlling the situation by nurturing, and she was able to open herself up to receive. As a result, she was able to let go of her underachieving staff and instead focus on what she loved to do most. She was also able to accept and receive assistance from those around her.

In fact, she now finds that people love to help her and she loves to receive. This allows her to move more into her feminine energy. She attracted a wonderful relationship where she does not feel compelled to coach her partner and instead was able to receive nurturing for herself and assistance for her business. This is particularly important now that she has a baby with her life partner!

# THE PRINCIPLE OF Creativity

## CHAPTER 4

# THE PRINCIPLE OF CREATIVITY

There was a time in our world when creativity was taking a back seat to logic and reason but now life is changing so rapidly that it has become imperative to innovate. People think of creativity as art but in fact creativity is really problem solving and adaptation. Without creativity there is no ability to think outside the box, find new solutions and therefore evolve.

I remember once seeing a miniseries about the brain and the narrator was talking about the difference between Neanderthals and Homo Sapiens. Over the tens of thousands of years that Neanderthals occupied the earth they created something like a hundred tools; over a much shorter period of time Homo sapiens produced more than 1500 tools. I have never been able to find that research again and it may be that with modern discoveries about prehistoric people these statistics are no longer accurate.

Nevertheless, it pointed out to me the importance of creativity in our ability to survive and thrive. It is quite clear that human beings are far more creative than other animals, and this capacity has allowed us to be a highly successful species. If we are to continue to overcome the problems of over-population, we will need to gain access to our creativity and innovation. Creativity is no longer a luxury – it has become necessary for survival.

### The Secret to Creativity is Imagination

Before you can create anything you need to be able to imagine it. As Albert Einstein famously said:

> "Imagination is more important than knowledge, for knowledge is limited to all we now know and understand, while imagination

embraces the entire world, and all there ever will be to know and understand."

Many people say to me: "But Pip, I am not imaginative or creative." So I ask them: "How did you come to be here today with me?" They usually answer, "Well I wanted to meet you and solve some of my problems." I ask, "And how did you know you wanted to come?" Then before they can catch themselves they usually answer something like: " Well, I imagined coming to see you and what results I could get. I didn't want to live like this anymore and I thought you could help me."

At this point the penny has usually dropped. You see, it is impossible to plan for the future, make decisions about what to do, drive, shop or function in any normal way without using the faculty of imagination.

People have this idea that imagination and creativity are limited to drawing, painting, music, acting and storytelling. If they are not talented in these things then they mistakenly believe they are unimaginative. The fact is that no problem solving is possible without imagination, even a simple problem like what to have for dinner, which movie to see or how to drive to work is impossible without imagination.

As far as creativity goes, I have seen some very creative ways that people create problems for themselves. I know people don't normally think of their problems as something they have created but in fact they are, and some problems take a great deal of time, effort, imagination and persistence.

Take smoking for example. In order to smoke someone has to have seen someone else smoke and then imagined themself doing the same. They also have to create positive associations to a very toxic, uncomfortable and stinky habit. They have to ignore all the physical realities of smoking and instead associate being a 'cool cowboy' or 'rebel' to continue this behaviour. It is interesting that people often associate smoking with being a rebel when in fact they are being obedient to a company's influence that wants to manipulate and destroy health for its own profit. They also have to deny all the health warnings and their body's own signals in order to continue smoking long enough to become addicted.

This is obviously a very negative use of imagination and creativity but I think if a smoker can do all of that they can create just about anything. This includes using the same imagination, creativity, persistence and ability to make positive associations in order to ignore physical withdrawal symptoms and overcome that same addiction to cigarettes.

The point is that you can use imagination and creativity to produce a wonderful life full of what you really want or you can use the same faculty to create problems and drama. Both use imagination and creativity, however the outcome depends on what you decide to create.

People often watch someone who is good at drawing and say, "Oh I wish I could draw like that." But they tend to ignore the huge amount of time, effort, focus and practice that person put in to become good at their art. If we spent the same amount of time perfecting that art, we may not be Michelangelo, but we would definitely be proficient at drawing.

This concept applies equally to business, relationship and health. If you are willing to put in the time, effort, concentration and persistence these things require you will be amazed at how you too will reap the rewards. Everyone is good at imagination and creativity, your current life is the result of that faculty. If you can create your life the way it is now, you can create it the way you want it using the same principle.

## The Creative Nurturer

There are some people who embody the Principle of Creativity. It is as if their ability to imagine and nurture images into being are a part of their artistic soul. Some of these people tend to be more creative and artistic while others are more nurturing and caring. Either way these people tend to be highly creative in one or more of the arts, writing, creating concepts or in the domestic arts, and/or business. They are also generally loving and caring of animals, nature and often children. They can be seen to represent the different aspects of the Universal Mother Archetype in all her guises, whether the person be male or female.

Think of people such as Oprah Winfrey, Andre Rieu, Nigella Lawson or John Goodman.

Oprah Winfrey is a perfect example of this Archetype. She has created an entirely new way of being a talk-show host with her empathetic style, which encourages open communication and emotional revelation. She is also exceptionally generous, giving away cars and countless donations, often to children's causes and those in need. She is incredibly nurturing of people's creativity, talents and emotions. To have a book endorsed by Oprah guarantees blockbuster status and Barack Obama gained approximately one million votes because of Oprah's endorsement.

Oprah's own childhood was filled with abuse and poverty. Her empathy comes from her own experiences of pain and her desire to see others given opportunities to heal. She used her own creativity and talent for communication and empathy to raise herself up to become a caring and successful example for others. This approach has made her the most influential woman on earth and also one of the wealthiest.

## Archetypal Creative Nurturers

All cultures have examples of the Creative Nurturer or Mother Archetype. One of my favourite examples of this is the Buddhist Goddess Guanyin. When, as a mortal, she gained enlightenment and was ascending to heaven she heard the lamentations of humanity. In her effort to comprehend their cries her head split into eleven pieces. Buddha, seeing her predicament, gave her eleven heads.

When she reached out to comfort all those she heard suffering, her arms shattered into a thousand pieces. Buddha then gave her a thousand arms so she could embrace all those in need.

She then vowed she would never ascend to heaven but stay on earth until all human suffering came to an end. Buddha then made her immortal and she became the Goddess of Mercy – the One Who Hears the Lamentations of the World. So she still resides here with us and is present in our hour of greatest need.

## My Experience

I was always a highly imaginative and creative child. So this Principle is one that came naturally to me. I always wanted to find a doorway to Narnia or sit on a wishing chair. I spent quite a bit of time stepping into likely cupboards or staring at pictures hoping they would turn into a portal to an imaginary world made real.

I also loved children and animals, and was one of those kids who was always picking up stray birds that had fallen out of nests and doing my best to nurture them back to health. I couldn't walk past a worm on a footpath without returning it to the soil – even to this day.

Children have always loved and trusted me, and one of my favourite things is to stop a young child crying in the street or on a plane by playing peek-a-boo. I spent a great deal of my childhood dressing up and acting out characters, and wanted to grow up to be a ballerina or actor. I also drew and wrote stories.

My dad was a great storyteller. When I was a child we used to go to my grandparents' place for the holidays and he would make up a story every night starring my brother and myself. One day he asked me to give him a subject that no one could possibly tell a story about. My father smoked cigarettes and was trying to cut down by rolling his own. I thought tobacco was pretty yucky so I chose Drum Tobacco as my challenge to my father. I thought no one could create a story about that!

My father then told the best story ever and I was mightily impressed. I came to the conclusion that if you were creative enough you could do anything and solve any problem. This belief had a profound effect on me. I still cherish this ideal today. It has created the foundation for my own work, as well as my love of great storytelling. I know I can create one out of any experience or about any subject matter. In fact when something negative happens I think, "Oh well, when I overcome this situation it is going to make a great story!"

 ### Your Turn

A lot of children have their imagination and creativity stifled by critical parents or through their own comparison to others but the fact is we are all creative beings and it is simply a matter of nurturing our unique internal imagination.

I find it is useful to go back to childhood to see if you can remember activities you enjoyed that were more creative. Did you like playing games, daydreaming or finger painting, or were you more into stories, music or singing?

Find a way to re-engage with your creativity. It may be as obvious as taking art, drawing, music, storytelling, creative writing or singing classes. Or you may decide to make up some stories to tell your kids, be more creative with cooking or some kind of craft.

You may want to rearrange your room or house to make it more visually appealing or create a vision board of your goals. Or simply sit down and imagine your perfect day and write a description of it through stream of consciousness.

One of my favourite creative activities is Morning Pages as outlined in the book *The Artist's Way* by Julia Cameron. The idea is to wake up in the morning and fill three A4 pages of stream-of-consciousness writing – which is just a fancy way of saying write down whatever comes into your mind, whether positive or negative, creative or repetitive. The idea is that when you siphon off the dross of your thinking, gems of creativity start to emerge from your subconscious mind. It also gets you into a habit of writing and not censoring yourself.

One of the tremendous bonuses of exploring your creativity is that it makes your whole mind more effective. When Albert Einstein had a particularly tricky problem he couldn't sort out, he would go into the basement and play the violin. After this he would be refreshed and was able to tackle the problem from a different angle and found it easier to explore solutions. Creativity and imagination are not a luxury we have when our work is done or we retire. It is essential to the everyday workings of the mind and imperative if we are to be productive, happy and successful.

## An Example of this Exercise

Years ago when I first came across *The Artist's Way* I was very inspired and decided to do Morning Pages religiously every morning. If for some reason I skipped a morning because I was too busy, I ensured I completed them before I went to sleep.

At the time I was quite frustrated and things in my life were not going the way I wanted. So, at first I have to admit, my Morning Pages were full of repetitive swear words. They would look something like this: F*&%, F*&%, F*&%, Sh!#@, Sh!#@, Sh!#@. You get the idea, I just want to illustrate the point that your Morning Pages are for your eyes only and you can write anything down. The point is NOT to censor yourself.

After a while of this and sentences like, "I don't know what to write. This is a silly exercise anyway! Why did I decide to do this", something amazing occurred – these negative thoughts began to fade away. It was as if they stopped going round and round in my head and began to empty out. I started to write long emotional explorations of what was really going on for me and possible solutions, which became extremely useful and therapeutic.

After about three weeks of doing the process I had another breakthrough. It was as if someone else was speaking to me. "I am Wind-in-Her-Hair. This is my story."

That sentence was the first step in the process of writing my first novel called *4 Tribes 1 Earth* and Wind-in-Her-Hair played a starring role!

## The Principle of Creativity applied to gaining Achievement, Love and Happiness

In this section I want to discuss an example from my partner, Will, instead of a client because it is so relevant to this subject. For years Will believed he had no imagination or creativity, even though he spent much of his childhood daydreaming and was an incredibly good problem solver.

He grew up in a poor Irish farming community where people generally stayed on the farm and followed what their parents had done. Everyone in the village was in the same boat growing up and there was very little variety or individuality among them. Families simply worked hard, survived and had a bit to drink to relax or maybe a lot to drink to escape.

Despite this Will, his brother and his sister came to Australia and made a better quality of life for themselves. The two brothers worked in their own business and did well. As a family they also invested in property very successfully. To me any immigrant has to have incredible powers of imagination to risk coming across the world to create a new life. Then to make it a success requires real creativity as well as a great deal of work and persistence.

When my partner had his first child she was highly artistic. She would constantly ask her father to draw or do something creative with her. He would reply: "But I don't have any imagination." She would then argue with him insisting that yes he did.

When I met him he still believed he had no imagination but despite this he was fascinated by my work and its practical applications and creativity. I decided it would not be healthy for our relationship to coach him, so I recommended one of my previous students, who is now a respected coach and a very good friend, to work with him.

He cleared the negative patterns passed down from his childhood by his parents and family and cleared the negative experiences he had at school and church. He also began to look at his Archetypes of Passion and Purpose, which is a unique way of discovering Passion and Purpose which I created based on The 8 Principles. After that he had a voracious appetite for learning more. He listened to all my CDs, read my previous books and decided to come to all of my Evolve Now! Level 1 courses, which he completed.

He realised his ability to problem-solve was indeed, based on his imagination. He even surprised me by renovating my bathroom while I was away in France. He did know what I wanted because I had been thinking of renovating my bathroom for about two years but it still took a great deal of imagination and creative problem-solving to complete the task.

Finally, he came to one of my Evolve Now! Level 2 advanced courses where we incorporate Horse Whispering as a way of further exploring

The Principles. At the time there was an activity using the Principle of Creativity to draw an impression of his profound experience with the horses. He still point-blank refused to do the exercise. I knew that putting any pressure on him would be counterproductive so I left it for another time.

A few days later, while I was busy coaching someone in the home office, Will was in the living room and he drew me a picture. He had been having some family issues that we had both been affected by and talked through. While I was working he had used a self-coaching technique he had learnt in one of my courses and then he drew a picture to acknowledge and thank me for my assistance. I was so moved by his gift that I cried. I knew how much it meant to him to overcome his issues with creativity to give me this gift and what a massive effort and shift it was. It was one of the most touching expressions of gratitude I have ever received. It revealed to me an even deeper secret hidden underneath The Principle of Creativity and that is the Power of Love.

# THE PRINCIPLE OF Organisation

**CHAPTER 5**

# THE PRINCIPLE OF ORGANISATION

While some people are so logical they cannot be creative, others lack the ability to use reason and logic to organise their thoughts and their life. Reason and creativity do not need to be mutually exclusive; they are both necessary for success. They are the king and queen of our capacity to think effectively and make decisions. We need to find ways for them to work in harmony if we are to achieve what we desire and be happy.

The key to using creativity and reason effectively is the sequence in which you use them. Creativity should always come first and then reason second, then you can create the best order for moving forward. This is why brainstorming when done properly is so effective. First, one needs to use imagination to come up with all the possible ideas or solutions without censorship or criticism. Then once all the ideas have been collected you use reason to order, prioritise and structure your ideas so they are appropriately organised. After all you cannot organise something you haven't yet created.

If you use reason first you cannot think outside the box. Reason is the capacity to look at everything inside the box and see if it is being used effectively or in the right sequence. It is imagination and creativity that allows us to think outside of the box. However, without reason to organise thoughts, life becomes chaotic and activities cannot be implemented effectively to create predictable outcomes. Organisation allows us to see causes and predict effects, which is the basis of all science. While it is fun to be spontaneous and explore, there are other times when we need to set goals or hypotheses, plan action and achieve outcomes. Both are necessary for success.

You may wonder what organisation has to do with love and happiness. When we are organised it is easier to have quality time to spend with our loved ones. It cuts through drama and panic and allows us to be less reactive and unreasonable. We have all had interactions with people who seem completely disorganised in their thinking and this does not make for effective communication or the ability to see someone else's point of view. Organisation and reason gives us the capacity to be calm and this allows us to notice when we are being unreasonable or unfair and make adjustments. It allows us to listen and weigh up what someone else is saying and make informed decisions. This type of communication develops trust and allows love and respect to flourish.

## The Secret to Organisation is Insight

Very few people realise how important insight is for proper organisation. When we say proper organisation we are not talking about being a 'control freak'. Obsessive control comes from the fact that someone is so out of control inside that they have to control everyone else and their environment. We are talking about real organisation that is the result of feeling at peace inside and having such keen insight into yourself and others that you can create the kind of structures that support creativity rather than suppress it.

It is like the difference between knowledge and wisdom. One is just a gathering of information the other is having the insight to know how to use that information.

So what exactly is insight? Insight is the ability to see beyond surface appearances to deeper meaning. It is the capacity to see below what someone is saying to their intention. It is the skill of seeing beyond immediate goals to a long-term vision. It is understanding behaviour in terms of its context, including personal, cultural and the era in which you find yourself. It is the capacity to think in structures and models without being boxed in by them but rather informed by them.

As you can see, insight takes us beyond following rules and into why the rules were created in the first place and if they are still relevant.

Insight allows us to see inside another human being and inside ourselves and accurately assess what is going on and then respond in a way that will create the best outcome. Insight gives us the capacity to be the best of who we are as a human being. It creates wise leadership and influences for the greatest good while taking into account individual needs and desires. It creates a complexity of thinking that is able to weigh up paradoxes and rise above them to create whole new paradigms of consciousness. It allows for different opinions to come together and have a positive impact on human evolution and endeavours.

## The Ruler

There are some people who embody the Principle of Organisation and order and we call these people Rulers. A ruler of course is a device that allows us to accurately measure and then organise things according to size. We use the term Ruler here to sum up this principle rather than it being the only concept of leadership. Any one of The Archetypes can be used as a form of leadership style. Where the Ruler was once the most dominant leadership style, there are now a large number of leaders who do not embody this persona and yet are incredibly successful. There has in fact been a shift away from this style, particularly as people have greater choices in the workplace and more autonomy.

Even those successful people who have a different kind of leadership style are going to need some kind of organisation to be effective. The leader who is totally disorganised and has not set up structures where systems can be put in place will soon lose control of an organisation.

In order to be a truly effective leader it is important that you develop, at least to an extent, all the skills of The 8 Principles. The wonderful thing about The 8 Principles is that it makes it easy to see what you do well and the strengths within your character, as well as what requires further work.

Having said that, there are of course many people who have been able to gain massive success by embodying the Principle of Organisation, along with its corresponding characteristics of strength and power.

Think of people such as Rupert Murdoch, Gina Rinehart, Hillary Clinton and Nelson Mandella.

Rupert Murdoch is a clear example of the Ruler. He is a powerful empire builder who is often described as 'owning the news'. He took over his father's Australian media company, News Limited, in the 1950s after his father's death. He was only 21 and very quickly began expanding the company by buying up struggling newspapers and turning them around financially. He went on to found News Corporation, which became the second largest media conglomerate after it took over newspapers in Australia, New Zealand, USA and the UK. He also acquired Mushroom Records and amalgamated it to create Festival Mushroom Records, as well as founding 21st Century Fox.

Although having supported Labor Politics in the early 1970s, he quickly changed his political affiliations and supported more conservative views. He did this when he wanted to strengthen his political affiliations in America to support his commercial holdings there. In the 1980s he acquired The Times and The Sunday Times in the UK which were struggling and he was able to turn them around. He is also the patriarch of a large family and has children from three marriages.

Murdoch is considered ruthless in his pursuit of power, wealth and influence and because of this some may think of him as a Shadow Ruler. No matter what you personally think of him there is no doubt he has a good head on his shoulders and is able to use reason to organise his empire in a logical way that supports growth and success.

## Archetypal Rulers

All cultures have examples of the Ruler Archetype, which is also an example of the Universal Father. When we think of the God of the Old Testament we have a concept of an all-powerful father figure whose rules and laws need to be obeyed in order to avoid punishment. With the New Testament we have a more forgiving and loving concept of God the Father. This is probably more in tune with modern and ideal concepts of a father who is insightful, kind and supportive.

Moses the lawgiver is a great archetypal example of the Ruler. He was insightful enough to work out how to free his people, then he had the strength, organisation and wisdom to ensure they lived. He ensured the Ten Commandment were provided to and obeyed by his people and this created simple guidelines that anyone could understand and a foundation for law and order.

It is important to remember what incredible powers of leadership Moses must have had. He convinced thousands of people to follow him out into the harsh desert and then was responsible for their survival and cooperation. This would have been particularly difficult when we remember that they had been slaves for centuries and knew what kind of punishment would be in store for them if they were ever recaptured.

> ## My Experience
>
> I was highly dyslexic as a child and didn't find it easy to sequence my thoughts or organise my room or my possessions. When I went to school I was always the kid who didn't have any pens and had forgotten to do my homework. I tended to use my creativity, improvisation and people skills to compensate and as a result they became highly developed.
>
> When I was in Year 9 I went to boarding school because my mum went to South-East Asia to complete her Master's degree. Boarding school was much more structured than my home life. We had to spend two hours every weekday in the library in silence doing our homework and one hour on Sunday.
>
> I remember being so bored I opened my homework diary for the first time outside of class. It may seem incredible but I had never before made the link between writing my homework down in my diary in class and then opening it up at home to remember what I had to do. It was a complete revelation.
>
> I started to do my homework, I started to read regularly and even write letters! By the end of Year 9 my marks had gone up an average of 40 per cent. My marks in maths went from about 54 per cent to a whopping 97 per cent – I couldn't believe it.
>
> I started to make friends with structure, order and planning which was very lucky because if I hadn't I would never have gained the marks to go to university or the tools to run a successful business. By the time I had finished university I was Dux of Sydney University for English teaching and won the PR Cole Memorial Prize for excellence. This is pretty incredible for someone who had so much trouble with spelling and reading as a child.
>
> I wouldn't say that structure, order and organisation are my favourite things to do in my business but I am so grateful I have those skills and I can think and analyse using logic and reason. It has meant I have been able to run a successful business doing what I love for the past 20 years.

# Your Turn

Sometimes when we have big goals we can find ourselves overwhelmed and this can cause us to procrastinate because we don't know where to start and how to prioritise.

This next exercise is from a process called the Hierarchy of Ideas in NLP. It is a wonderful way to use the Principle of Organisation to overcome procrastination. It will assist you in taking action on what is logically the most important place to start. It allows your mind to be laser focused because you have no doubt about what is most important.

**Step 1:** Write down in the centre of a piece of paper the words: 'My Life'. Then underneath all the areas of your life that you currently feel overwhelmed by. It could be 'my business', 'my house' or 'my kids'. I know you will probably want to answer, 'everything', but resist the urge and pick specific areas.

**Step 2:** Underneath one area heading write down all the subsections which overwhelm you. For instance, in business it could be marketing, sales targets, administration, book-keeping and presentations.

**Step 3:** Pick what is most important to your business goals – it could be marketing. Now underneath the heading 'marketing' write down the subsections of marketing you feel overwhelmed about, it could be email, web pages or social media.

**Step 4:** Then choose the most important one to your business success right now: For example web pages. Write down the tasks you need to accomplish in that subsection. It might be writing web copy, making sure links are live or making sure the shopping cart works.

**Step 5:** Repeat the process with other important areas of your business.

**Step 6:** Work out what is your most important task by comparing tasks to your business goals and your time frames. Look at what you can delegate and what you need to do yourself. Work out exactly what you need to do now and then write in your diary the dates other important tasks need to be completed by.

**Step 7:** Take action on your chosen task confident in the understanding you are doing what is most important.

Now repeat the process with other areas of your life.

This is a tremendously effective process and leads to very efficient action. It also allows you to instantly see what outcomes are dependent on particular activities without the complexity of a Gant Chart.

## An Example of this Exercise

Recently, I went to Africa and donated some money to a poor village to build a piggery. A truly amazing priest supervised the project. He was very proactive and full of great ideas to improve the villages in his parish.

We were talking about different concepts of what to do next and he had many great ideas but it wasn't easy to see which would be the priority.

In the end I asked him for a piece of paper and we performed this exercise. We looked at all the major problems in the village, such as a lack of running water, no school, no employment, no industry and no sustainable income.

We looked at all the ways he was building sustainable income, like growing bananas and sweet potatoes and breeding chickens and pigs. We looked at what the pigs and chickens needed, which was milled corn, coffee husks, sweet potato greens and water.

At first we were looking at providing running water for both the people and the animals but to solve that problem would take a lot more money than we could currently access.

As we looked more closely at the outline the priest realised that a corn mill was the most important thing for the village. You see the villages grew a lot of corn and had to take it to town to get it milled. This was time consuming and cost money in petrol and car hire as the majority of the villagers didn't own a car.

The priest himself was having large amounts of corn milled to feed the baby chickens and the pigs so he had to hire a truck to take the corn into town.

What we worked out was that setting up a corn mill would save him large amounts of money and bring money into the village because the ten surrounding villages could bring their corn to be milled in his village instead of town. That would save them money in petrol and car hire. It was so exciting. Especially when we realized that when people came to get their corn milled they would probably want something to eat and drink as well and this could provide added income.

We then sat down and worked out the savings and earnings. We saw the mill would pay for itself within two to three months. So this was definitely the priority and we would never have seen this solution if it wasn't for that exercise. In fact money from the sales of this book went to that village to fund that project. The great news is that with the ongoing use of this simple tool my friend can always check what is the greatest priority. The added bonus is that he can easily communicate that to the people who want to support him.

## The Principle of Organisation applied to gaining Achievement, Love and Happiness

I had a client who was a very successful businessman and had millions of dollars. When he came to me he said that even if he really tried he would never be able to spend all the money he had earned.

He had spent years building up his business working incredibly long hours, being very disciplined and structured. Then he sold his business for a huge amount of money and for three years he did absolutely nothing. For the first six months he really enjoyed himself. He sailed, he played golf and hung at the beach feeling very happy with himself and thinking about all those people who had to be at work.

After a while however his early retirement began to wear thin. He didn't like doing activities by himself and all his friends were at work during the day. It would really get to him by about 3pm and then he would open a bottle of wine or two. Then the next day he'd be tired. By the time he found me he was beginning to feel mildly depressed but knew it was somehow self-imposed. He didn't want to start up another business because he didn't want to get sucked back in to his old workaholic behaviour, particularly when he didn't like the person he became when he was stressed. He wanted to maintain his freedom but ironically his desire for completely unstructured freedom had become a trap.

He also wanted to get fit but found himself afraid even to commit to this as a discipline.

So we looked at what he had loved to do as a child, teen and adult. We compared that to The 8 Principles and from there were able to discover his Archetypal Passion and Purpose. We were then able to work with his desire for freedom, creativity and achievement to find a new structure to his day, business and future goals that were more fluid, fun and inviting.

His work became assisting others to make their Passion and Purpose an achievable business reality. This allowed him to go in and out of many businesses without getting bogged down in the details or the day-to-day running of them. He could pick and choose his projects and the people he worked with. He set up a charity for middle-aged men who had lost direction but had fantastic expertise and connected them with start-ups. I also connected him with a lovely personal trainer who was fun and creative and he then found himself exercising every day.

He has now set up a charitable organisation that funds worthy projects and start-ups. I had lunch with him recently in an organic café he had supported as a start up. He was really happy and felt his life had meaning again. He was also making a substantial contribution to the world and solving major social problems people face.

With insight we were able to work with his personality, passion and purpose to create structures that supported who he really was. This is where the Secret of Insight became so powerful. Most people use reason to create structures that box people in rather than finding the structures that allow people to flourish. This was the key to this principle – and what makes for truly fantastic fathering – creating structures that support children to flourish and develop their unique genius.

He had also made some tough decisions to leave his previous partner. Two years later he had found a wonderful woman who shared his fun-loving personality and desire for adventure.

# THE PRINCIPLE OF Intuition

## Chapter 6

# THE PRINCIPLE OF INTUITION

Truly effective intuition is beyond reason but not counter to it. Usually intuition is a process by which you know something accurately without understanding exactly how you came to that conclusion.

Generally, people have their most accurate intuition about a subject they have expertise in. It is that flash of brilliance which brings everything together. However, without the previous study or experience that flash of brilliance could not happen or would not be based on a solid foundation. This is why even a court of law is willing to allow the opinion of an expert. They are more likely have accurate intuition about someone and their behaviour or intention, even if they were not present.

The phenomenon of intuition is likely to come as a result of the hidden workings of the unconscious mind. Professor Allan Snyder at the Centre for the Mind at Sydney University believes the subconscious mind, or as he calls it, the 'other than conscious mind', is about 96 per cent of the mind's capacity and the conscious mind then is about 4 per cent of the mind's capacity.

This means the subconscious mind is picking up and absorbing much more information than the conscious mind is. The subconscious mind also has access to all your memories and previous experiences. John Grinder, of NLP fame, believes the subconscious mind binds all this together and comes to a conclusion, which it presents to the conscious mind at important moments. You are therefore not consciously aware of how you came to a specific conclusion.

The benefit of intuition is that it is very fast and can allow you to make snap decisions. The downside is that sometimes we can be convinced of things that have less to do with intuition and more to do with fear or desire. The key to accurate intuition is the ability to hear the difference between intuition and emotion. The other thing that interrupts intuition is an over-reliance on logic. Logic is limited to all that is known or conclusions made from a known premise. But what if the original premise is incorrect or there are too many variables to account for logically?

Intuition allows us to make leaps into the unknown and draw accurate conclusions from the profound. Unfortunately, many people will dismiss this inner knowing because they cannot make sense of it then later lament saying: "I knew I should have followed my intuition!" This statement comes from the certainty of hindsight. Following Intuition instead allows us to make rapid decisions in the uncertainty of the moment, so it is definitely a faculty worth developing and trusting.

## The Secret to Intuition is Listening

The ancients called intuition the 'still, quiet voice', and it was often accessed through meditation or prayer. They believed that through the pathway of the subconscious mind the higher self could communicate with you. As a result, they had a more spiritual concept of intuition than the psychological version outlined above. This would explain the kind of intuition that is more in line with psychic phenomenon and comes to someone with no prior knowledge, experience or expertise.

This would explain the type of intuition experienced by someone such as Joan of Arc, who was able to have such incredible intuition, belief, and faith that she could lead whole armies to victory without any prior experience. There are dozens of examples in history and legend about this kind of intuition. For most people however intuition is a bringing together of experience and knowledge into subconscious understanding that is communicated through a gut feeling or a sense of knowing. I call this 'everyday intuition' because it is something practical that everyone can develop and is most prevalent in areas of the person's expertise.

Either way in order to follow your intuition you need to be able to listen to it and discern when it is real. Even a gut feeling or vision still has to be understood and its message listened to in order to be useable.

## The Sage

There are some people who embody the Principle of Intuition and we call these people the Sage. Sages tend to be fascinated by a particular area of knowledge and then able to access something higher and more profound than the learnings they have acquired. This allows them to pioneer new ways of thinking and inventing.

Think of people such as Marie Curie, Albert Einstein, Steve Jobs and Naomi Wolf.

Marie Curie was the Polish/French physicist and chemist who conducted pioneering research on radioactivity. She was the first woman to win a Nobel Prize and the only person to win it twice in multiple disciplines.

She came from a family of intellectuals who became poverty stricken because of their political beliefs. Yet Marie continued to tutor herself and fund her way through the University of Paris even though she was often cold and faint with hunger.

She intuitively came up with the hypothesis that radiation was not the outcome of an interaction of molecules, as previously thought, but came from the atom itself. This incredible intuitive leap disproved the ancient theory that atoms were indivisible and was an important first step in her pioneering work. She also discovered and named radium and its effects on tumour-forming cells. She coined the term radiation. During the First World War she set up mobile X-rays and radiation units which treated and saved hundreds of wounded soldiers.

## Archetypal Sage

All cultures have examples of the Sage Archetype. One of my favourite Archetypal Sages is Chiron, the centaur from Greek mythology. Chiron's father was Kronus who was caught by his wife in the act of having sex with the nymph Philyra. He disguised himself by turning into a horse. The resulting child was half-human half-horse. When Philyra gave birth she was horrified by the child's appearance and abandoned him.

The God of Light, Apollo, took pity on the babe and brought him up teaching him all he knew about the arts, music, medicine, herbs and philosophy. Chiron continued to study these disciplines himself and became the mentor of all the great heroes such as Ajax, Theseus, Achilles, Jason and Heracles. In the end he was mortally wounded by an arrow but because he could not die he remained in intense pain until he sacrificed his immortality for the life of Prometheus.

Chiron is best known as the wounded healer. We can see this played out in many historic and real life examples of Sages. For example, Marie Curie died from the effects of the very radium she used to save lives during the First World War.

> ## My Experience
>
> I have never been so fascinated or spent so much joyous time studying anything as I have The Principles and the Archetypal figures associated with them. I think it is because they are so applicable to everyday life and they help me understand human behaviour and motivation at such a deep, profound level.
>
> One of the things I love about The Principles is how they help to deepen my intuitive capacity. It has made a massive difference to my coaching and my trainings. It becomes easier to predict other's needs and behaviours and to see what is going on for them under surface appearances. This has given me a point of difference that my clients recognise and is part of the reason they recommend me.
>
> In my own life I have also had tremendous benefit from following my intuition. It means that I have been able to predict future trends and understand what direction society is heading. This allows me to understand the issues people will face and then pioneer processes that will assist in problem-solving.
>
> That does not mean I have not made mistakes in my life or my business, but the mistakes are due to ignoring The Principles instead of following them. One of the benefits of knowing The Principles is that you can learn so much more quickly from your mistakes and create more empowering behaviours instead of repeating the same old patterns again and again.
>
> One of the great things about intuition is it allows you to trust your own judgment and make decisions more quickly and with greater confidence.

 **Your Turn**

The two greatest obstacles that prevent people following intuition are: emotions, such as desire and fear, and false logic. For example, you may have a desire to 'not make a fuss', or have a fear of 'missing out' that might interrupt your intuition. Or you may have listened to false logic telling you that of course everything would be all right when it is obviously not and this can prevent you from listening to a greater truth.

Emotions and false logic often interrupt intuition in relationships which you know are not right for you. People stay longer in toxic relationships than they should because they are afraid of being alone or hurting the other person. They then justify staying by using false logic such as: "I won't find anyone else at my age, so I might as well stay." The fact is that plenty of people at any age find new relationships, if they just give themselves a chance and free themselves from critical or abusive partners.

One of the easiest ways to help your ability to hear your intuition clearly is to calm down the voices of emotion and false logic. So when you have a decision to make and you are not sure if you are really following your intuition or not, then use this exercise.

Firstly, write down all your fears and desires about the subject on a piece of paper. This allows your emotions to feel heard and understood. Then write down what logic and reason say, this allows that part of your mind to feel like you are being sensible.

Next, put both pieces of paper aside and imagine emotion and logic kneeling and surrendering control to intuition.

Imagine intuition as the Sage Archetype pictured at the beginning of this chapter. Imagine stepping into this picture and stepping into the body of the Sage. Really feel like you are the Sage.

See your emotions represented by the woman in the picture and logic represented as the man kneeling before you.

Now as the Sage feel as though you can truly access your intuition and wisdom and ask for the real solution to the problem. Then write down your answer from the Sage's point of view. Your answer may come immediately or it may come later when you are in the shower or going for a walk. What is important is that you have set the intention of gaining an answer from the Sage; your internal mentor who is actually your higher self.

## An Example of this Exercise

One of the most powerful experiences I have had with intuition was with my horse. We run a series of residential programs in country New South Wales using all of *The 22 Principles of Success* (this book covers the first 8 of those Principles). At that program we work with a herd of horses to deepen people's understanding and experience of the Principles, using horse whispering. As prey animals, horses are seven times more perceptive than humans because they need to be aware of their environment and predators to survive. Horses have a heightened awareness for incongruences between appearances and real intentions because they have to be able to sense when a predator is on the prowl or when it is simply getting a drink of water from a shared waterhole. A predatory animal basically pretends that it is not hunting by crouching and hiding and a prey animal needs to be able to sense them and their intentions so they can survive. As a result horses, with their heightened awareness, act as a reflection of a person's internal incongruencies and often can asist humans to access their own emotional truth.

Years ago a boyfriend of mine had given me a horse, which was an ex-pacer and she was always running around with her tail held high in the air. I was so excited to receive her because I had wanted a horse since I was six years old. In fact my full name, Philippa, means "lover of horses". So it was a dream come true for me and I was very grateful to him.

She was kept on his farm and used as a weaning mare but because we had broken up I hadn't seen her for a while. One day when I was on the way to the program I had the most intense need to see my horse. As I hadn't seen my ex for years, I felt a deep desire not to intrude on his land and this was compounded by the fact I had my current life-partner with me, so it was a very awkward situation.

My emotions were screaming at me not to go and false logic was telling me I was being silly and that everything was all right with the horse. What was wrong with me? Was I trying to sabotage my new relationship?

I sat for a moment listening to everything my emotions and logic were telling me. Then I pictured being the Sage and I listened for the deep, quiet voice of intuition. My intuition was quite clear; no matter how uncomfortable it felt I needed to see my horse immediately. So my current partner and I went. I have learnt from bitter experience not to ignore my intuition.

When I arrived I found that my horse could barely walk. She was foundering. Her hooves were beginning to look like slippers and she was obviously finding it painful to even put one foot in front of the other. I was devastated. My mother had lost her own horses to foundering when she was a young woman, so I knew it could be fatal and a very painful way for a horse to die. It was especially frightening for a horse like mine which was so flighty and liked to run.

I came back to where I was staying and did my best to contact my ex and a farrier. We found out that my ex had been away earning money to support his farm. Also, my horse had very fast-growing and incredibly hard hooves, which the old farrier had not been able to cut.

As it turned out, the very next day a barefoot farrier was coming to where I was staying to look after some other horses on the property. Interestingly, when I spoke to her she had just had a cancellation that day.

We were able to go to my horse and two and half hours later with three people's help we were able to sort out her feet. In the end there was a final closure between my ex and myself and this meant my new partner and I were able to become even closer. I then organized for the farrier to look after my horse's feet and everyone was happy.

I am very grateful that, despite the awkwardness of the situation, I followed my intuition when it really mattered. A year later my horse suddenly passed away and I was terribly saddened but I was grateful that I had been able to make sure her final months were happy and pain free.

## The Principle of Intuition applied to gaining Achievement, Love and Happiness

I worked with a client who was in a very toxic relationship. He was a lovely man who was intelligent, funny and kind but he was married to someone who was incredibly critical and difficult to get on with. When he came to me he really wanted to end the relationship but was too afraid. His self-esteem and self-confidence were very low. He was also, understandably, worried about his children and how the break-up would affect them.

It was clear however that his children were already being affected by the incredible strain in the household. The client's mother-in-law was also living in the house and there was a ganging up against the father, particularly when he wanted to spend time with his boys. The mother-in-law was encouraging childish behaviour in the kids who were beginning to be teenagers and needed to take on board more responsibility and maturity. In the meantime the father's opinion was rarely listened to or respected.

As we talked further it became clear the client was repeating almost exactly the same scenario as his parents. His mother was very dominating and critical and his father was, as he described him, a big teddy bear.

As the coaching progressed we cleared the negative influence of both his mother and father using my Matrix Therapies® Coaching. We also cleared his fears. We then looked at all the positives and negatives of staying or leaving. He looked at the benefit to his boys of leaving and how he could provide a home where they learnt greater independence. Even if they went home to the same behaviour with their mother and grandmother they could at least gain skills and maturity in an alternative home.

We discussed how the purpose of coaching was not to make him stay or leave but for him to be free to make the decision that was right for him and to give him more choices. He became more assertive at home and this made a massive difference to his self-esteem and self-respect but it didn't change the situation. We talked about seeking legal advice so he could be more informed. We also wrote out the intuition exercise described previously in the *Your Turn* section of this book.

A little while after that he came to me really excited. He had left his wife and home and had set up a new apartment. He had seen the solicitor. I asked him what had changed and he said: "I suddenly had this feeling that I had to leave right then. It didn't make much logical sense but I knew it was the right thing to do. So I just did it."

He found out later that his wife was planning to leave him the very next day. He said he was so pleased he followed his intuition because he felt it was his decision and he could be proactive in changing his circumstances. He said he was incredibly grateful that we had cleared all the negative programming of his parents and the emotions associated with them because otherwise he would not have been able to hear and follow his intuition. Previously his judgment was clouded by indecision but now he felt he had absolute clarity.

From there his life has gone from strength to strength. His business became far more successful, he has become fit and healthy, he has been dating and he said he has a newfound feeling of freedom and confidence. He said he was amazed at how positively women responded to him.

What he loves most however is the connection he has with his kids. He said to me: "I feel so proud that I can be a worthy mentor to my teenage boys and help them understand what it means to be a good, kind, confident and respected man."

# THE PRINCIPLE OF Discernment

## CHAPTER 7

# THE PRINCIPLE OF DISCERNMENT

Discernment is the ability to make correct assessments of a situation without reactivity and then take appropriate action. If you can discern effectively you can cut away what is not accurate or important. You can also create useful boundaries. It is not always easy to make decisions when there are so many different influences on us. There is however a lode star that can light our way and allow us to make outstanding decisions.

### The Secret to Discernment is Self-Love

When we love ourselves we can make decisions that come from security and self-esteem, rather than fear and reactivity. When we ask, "what is the most self-loving thing I can do in this situation", we are able to cut through the fog of confusion and find clarity. Many people think self-love is the same as selfishness but they are completely different. When we make decisions that come from selfishness the decisions we make benefit us at the detriment of others. When we love ourselves the decisions we make are best for us and the greater good. Even if these decisions cause pain and hurt to begin with – in the end they are for the best.

I don't know if you have ever had a friend talk to you about someone they really want to break up with but can't seem to bring themselves to do it. Usually they say something like: "Oh, I don't like him any more, but I can't break up with him. I don't want to hurt him."

The fact is she is hurting him every day she stays because by staying she is preventing him from finding someone who really loves him and wants to be with him. In actual fact it is selfish to stay with someone you don't want to be with. If your friend asked herself the question;

"what is the most self-loving thing I can do in this situation", she would soon break up with her boyfriend. He may feel rejected and hurt in the short term but at least he is now free to find someone else and she is not wasting his time.

## The Lovers

People who love themselves usually find loving partners and have successful relationships. We call people who embody this Principle The Lovers. If someone can use this Principle effectively then they are discerning about the partner they choose and create a long-term loving relationship that support their dreams and brings out the best in each other.

Think of couples such as Hugh Jackman and Deborra-Lee Furness, Melinda and Bill Gates, Martin Luther and Coretta King and Joanne Woodward and Paul Newman.

Hugh Jackman and Deborra-Lee Furness have had a successful, loving relationship that has lasted 20 years and counting. They believe that good communication and friendship are the bedrock of their relationship. Hugh adds romance by surprising his wife and by ensuring they are never apart for more than two weeks. Deborra says it is easy to grow apart if you are away from each other for longer than that.

Hugh credits his wife for his confidence and success as an actor. He believes he has become infinitely braver and more within himself from being with his wife. He believes he has learnt a great deal from her.

She, in turn, has contributed to changes in adoption laws in Australia.

Here we see a wonderful example of the Lovers in the light. Hugh and Deborra are a couple who love and respect each other. Their relationship supports their passion and purpose and adds another dimension to their contributions to the world.

## The Lovers in Shadow

If this Principle is not used effectively people can instead use relationships to escape from internal pain. When couples do this they become co-dependent. Their relationship takes over their life. Instead of loving themselves they try to compensate for a lack of self-esteem by filling themselves with their partner's love and attention.

Unfortunately, this creates further insecurity because now their self-esteem is based on someone else. This can then lead to jealousy and a need to control the other person to ensure their attention. Relationships like this become very destructive; the partner feels that anything that takes away their lover's attentiveness is a 'bad' thing. As a result the partner loses connection with family, friends and passions.

The antidote to co-dependence is self-love. When an individual loves themselves they are not dependent on their partner for their sense of self. A partner adds a new dimension to the person's life rather than *being* their life. This is what creates healthy relationships and couples then have the space and confidence to support each other's dreams.

## Archetypal Lovers

All cultures have examples of the Lovers Archetype. My favourite positive example of this Archetype is Sir Gawain and the Lady of Little Mercy of twelfth century literature. When they first meet Gawain is a philanderer and the Lady is embittered because of her own past tragedy.

To begin with the Lady is disdainful and tests Gawain mercilessly, hence her name. Gawain sees the Lady as simply another conquest to feed his inflated ego. As their relationship develops however they are able to be vulnerable, heal their wounds and discover self-love and self-respect.

As a result they can find true and lasting love with each other. It is incredible how a 12th century story can be so relevant today. When themes are archetypal and elucidate The Principles they have a lasting truth that transcends time and culture.

## My Experience

The Principle of Discernment and Self-Love was one that took me a long time to master. Considering my childhood abuse from a family 'friend' and the death of my father, it is no wonder I found this not easy. However, what I have discovered from coaching hundreds of people is that most people struggle with this concept even if they have not experienced any trauma.

It is very common for children to grow up feeling like they are not good enough or somehow unlovable. Kids often misinterpret criticism and parental frustration with being unloved.

When I decided I wanted a relationship I wasn't discerning about who I chose. My pattern was to find a man who was wounded who I thought my love could heal. I was not thinking about loving myself and finding a person who would love me in a positive way, instead I was completely caught up with the other person's needs.

In a deep subconscious part of my mind I thought if I healed someone they would need me and then not leave me. Obviously this is false logic and not very conducive to a positive relationship. You can't make someone love you because of something you give them and ultimately people heal themselves anyway.

I decided to focus on this area of my life. It was painful; I had wanted to ignore it because it was one of the few places where I felt a failure. For a long time I pretended I didn't really want a partner. I was in fact very independent and happy in my career but there came a point where I had to admit the truth – I wanted to share my life with someone I loved and who loved me back.

I realised that if I wanted to really solve this issue I needed to look at The 8 Principles of Achievement, Love and Happiness and apply them specifically to my love life. It was interesting because even though I knew The Principles I had been resisting applying them to my relationships. Below are the steps I took to gain love I was searching for.

1. Principle of Energy, Secret of Inspiration: I needed to be inspired to have a relationship and the energy to begin searching. So I looked

around at friends who had successful relationships and asked them how they met and what they enjoyed about being in a relationship.

2. Principle of Concentration, Secret of Focus: I focused on ensuring that having a relationship was a priority in my life.

3. Principle of Receptivity, Secret of Vulnerability: I looked at my ability to receive and feel vulnerable. This was a big problem for me. I didn't feel in control when I received and this made me feel frightened.

   I did a lot of work on this area, both in Therapeutic Coaching and in practising receiving with grace, whether that was a compliment, help or a present. I practised receiving without obligation to give back. I began to understand the way you receive a present is a gift in and of itself.

   I also let people know I wanted a relationship. This also made me feel vulnerable but after all if no one knew what I wanted they would not be able to help me.

4. Principle of Creativity, Secret of Imagination: I began to imagine what it would be like to be in an ideal relationship and what that would mean to me. I also started to nurture myself, giving myself time to relax, getting massages and doing creative things I loved.

5. Principle of Organisation, Secret of Insight: I started to look carefully at the men I met or dated. Instead of wondering if they would like me or not, I began to check if they really had the character to be in the type of relationship I wanted. If they didn't I learned to create boundaries and to stop seeing them. One of my big fears about dating was saying 'No' to someone I didn't want to see again. I really didn't want to reject anyone or hurt their feelings.

   My coach told me about a friend of his who went on a date with a man. At the end of the date the man said: "It has been really lovely meeting you, I enjoyed spending time together and you are a great person. The thing is, I am looking for my life-partner and I don't feel like we have that kind of connection. So I want to spend all my time looking for that person. All the very best with your search."

   His friend said at first she was miffed. After that however she felt grateful. She didn't have to wait around wondering if the phone was going to ring or wonder if she should ring him. She said it was fantastic she knew exactly where she stood. She didn't have to waste any time and could get on with finding someone else. She also had a great line to say at the end of a date if she wasn't interested.

I also thought it was fantastic. It was an incredibly mature and respectful way of saying no. I used the line myself. It made it much easier to face a date because I felt I could be honest at the end and not string someone along simply because I didn't know what to say. This helped me organise my time and put myself in dating situations.

6. Principle of Intuition, Secret of Listening: Intuition and listening to myself was also incredibly important. I did start dating someone during this journey. He was a great guy who I liked a lot but my intuition kept saying he wasn't right for me. In the end I listened to myself and broke up with him. A number of months later I briefly connected with him again and it became clear to me my intuition had been completely correct. Even before I had all the information I needed to make an informed decision my intuition had already come to the right conclusion. It was great I had listened to myself and we were able to part on good terms.

7. Principle of Discernment, Secret of Self-Love: The two previous Principles went a long way to building my self-esteem. Being able to say no to someone in a respectful way, because it wasn't right for me, and listening to my intuition gave me a sense of self-worth. The more I healed my past experiences and learned to love myself to a greater degree the better my discernment became. I could feel my internal development in this area was opening me up more and more to finding the right person. It was incredible. I felt I could become more vulnerable and feminine in a way that was strong and appealing. I could feel my heart blossoming – it was a wonderful feeling.

8. Principle of Results, Secret of Action. During this process of going through the 8 Principles of Achievement I asked a friend how she had found her partner. She told me all about it. She asked me if I was looking for a partner. I said I was. She said she knew someone who would be perfect and did I like Irish men. Of course I did, who doesn't!

# CHAPTER 7 – THE PRINCIPLE OF DISCERNMENT

> She said she would get back to me. Months went by, I totally forgot about our conversation. Instead I continued practicing the 8 Principles and working on myself. After doing all that work I simply surrendered, I remember saying to the sky one night: "You know exactly who would be right for me, find him for me." Some people might call that putting it out to the universe, others would call it praying or surrendering. It doesn't really matter how we make sense of it, in the end it is letting go of control and trusting in something greater.
>
> Three days later my friend rang me to say the Irishman she had in mind had boken up with the woman he had dated briefly. He had declared to her: "That's it! I never want to be in a relationship again. I am over it. I will just have to live my life alone." He was expecting to get sympathy from her as his best friend. Instead she said: "Great I am so happy you broke up with her because I have the perfect person for you."
>
> He was very reluctant to try dating again after his declaration but eventually he rang me. We went on a date and then another and another over six weeks. After that we realised we were meant for each other and have been together ever since.

Note: People talk about the Principle of Surrender, which is one of The 7 Principles of Growth (the subject of the next book), but many people don't realise that without the other steps to support it, surrender is merely giving up responsibility. With the other steps in place surrender means you have done everything you can and now it's time to trust it will come to you at the right moment.

### Your Turn

Think about something you want that you haven't managed to achieve yet. Take a moment to go inside and ask yourself: "Do you really believe you are worthy of having what you most desire?"

If not, look at what beliefs are holding you back.

Look at how these beliefs are stopping you from getting what you want. Ask how you would behave if you did not accept those old beliefs.

Start acting as if those beliefs are not true for you. Ask yourself what new beliefs would support your goals. Act as if these beliefs are true for you.

Look at how you can treat yourself in a way that shows self-love in this area of your life and is the opposite of those old limiting beliefs.

Review The Principles, as in my example above, and apply them to your life.

Allow yourself to be vulnerable and ask for help if you need it. That may be from a coach to clear away past fears and negative beliefs or it could be from friends or mentors who can give you resources or excellent advice.

Finally, take action and put yourself out in the world. This is the final Principle of Achievement and is the subject of the next chapter.

## An Example of this Exercise

Usually I give an example here but I think the example I gave in My Experience above covers this Principle thoroughly.

## The Principle of Discernment applied to gaining Achievement, Love and Happiness

One time I had a couple come to me. The woman really wanted to take her relationship to the next level and wanted to get married and have children but her partner wasn't sure if that was what he wanted.

We spent time looking at his parents' relationship both with each other and with him. His father was an abusive alcoholic and treated his mother very badly. At some point he had vowed he would never turn into his father but unconsciously he was terrified he would. He hated the part of himself that reminded him of his father. The way he had avoided becoming the father he hated was by ensuring he would never become a father.

The thing was however he loved his girlfriend and he wanted to get married and begin a family, particularly as they were now well into their thirties.

We started coaching and helped him disconnect from the influence of his father. He was able to see that even if he had some of his father's qualities that did not mean he was his father.

He was able to see himself as his own person capable of making his own decisions. He was able to love himself as the man that he was and see that he would, in truth, make a wonderful father.

That night after his coaching session about his father he went home and proposed to his girlfriend. His ability to love himself, despite his upbringing allowed him to discern what he truly wanted. He realised he could truly love and be loved in return.

That couple have been happily married for years now and have two beautiful children. He is a wonderful supportive husband and father.

# THE PRINCIPLE OF Results

**CHAPTER 8**

# THE PRINCIPLE OF RESULTS

The best results are the outcomes you gain by achieving the goals you have set. Few people really understand that we all get results no matter what we do because results are the end product of behaviour. The question is are you getting the results you want? And just as important, are the results you are getting making you happy?

Sometimes people put a great deal of effort into getting results only to find that what they thought they wanted didn't give them the feeling they were expecting.

If you do not get the outcomes you desire it is important to trace back the beliefs, emotions and influences that led to your behaviour and make changes in these areas. Our behaviour is simply the external outcome of our internal processes and the actions we take.

In order to get what we want we need to follow the first 7 Principles of Achievement but in the end we must take action to be successful.

## The Secret to Results is Action

Anyone who has achieved anything in life knows the secret to getting results is taking action. This secret is probably the most obvious of all but the key is taking the *kind* of action that leads towards a successful outcome.

It is incredible how often people take action that leads them away from what they want rather than towards it. This is often due to feeling unworthy of achievement and sabotaging success. Or people are afraid of criticism so do not want to put themselves out there where others may judge them.

Without taking action it is not possible to get what you want. One of the downfalls of the movie *The Secret* was the suggestion that focusing on what you want was enough by itself. It promoted the idea that if you focused on what you wanted strongly enough that things would magically appear.

It is possible you may get what you want in this way – less than one per cent of the time – but if you require the consistent achievement that creates success, then you must take the action required.

Focus and concentration are of course incredibly important because of the way they train your mind to notice your goal and the people and things that will help you get it. To know what you want is the most important second step towards achievement but without taking action you will not achieve success.

What the Principles of Achievement shows us is that action is the final step to getting what you want. Action also means taking what you have created out into the world and contributing it to others.

## The Knight

There are some people who embody the Principle of Results and we call these people Knights. Knights are action takers. Unlike the Innocent Adventurer who is also energetic, the Knight has a goal and purpose in mind that drives their behaviour. They want to achieve and when happy are highly motivated, determined and goal orientated. They may be sporty but their drive may be entrepreneurial or humanitarian.

Think of people such as Mahatma Gandhi, Mother Teresa, Muhammad Ali and Cathy Freeman.

Even though Gandhi is often referred to as the Father of the Nation, archetypally he is a Knight. He was the leader of the Indian movement for independence against British rule but he never took up the office of government, like Nelson Mandela did. Both have knight-like qualities, particularly in their protest years but Mandela also had the Ruler as a major archetype.

Gandhi preferred to remain outside of government to be free to influence without a political agenda and also to lead by example. He led campaigns to ease poverty, expand women's rights, build religious and ethnic amity and end untouchability – but most of all he is remembered for achieving self-rule for India.

He was imprisoned many times in his efforts to champion those who were disempowered. He advocated non-violence and truth in all situations. He was an inspiring example for the civil rights movement and for millions of people around the world who believe we should all "be the change you want to see in the world".

## Archetypal Knight

My favourite Archetypal Knight is Parzival, and his quest for the Holy Grail.

At first Parzival happens across the Grail by accident but he is naïve so he doesn't understand its value nor the questions he is required to ask to obtain it. As a result the Grail is lost to him and the land remains barren.

When he realises what he has done he bitterly regrets his failings. He then vows to search for the Grail, sacrificing love and comfort until he finds it. Interestingly however you cannot find the Grail when you seek it. That is one of its mysteries.

In the end Parzival becomes so depressed by his failure that he lets the reins of his horse drop and his horse leads him into the deepest, darkest part of the forest where he meets a Wise Hermit. The Hermit takes Parzival on an internal journey where he heals the wounds passed on to him by his mother and father and discovers his true identity.

When he has finished he leaves the forest and the Grail Castle magically appears before him. Because of his internal journey he is now prepared and can ask the Fisher King the correct questions. This releases the King from his pain and allows the Grail to heal the land.

Parzival is then magically reunited with his wife and all is well.

All Knights go on this archetypal journey. They search for fulfillment, satisfaction and happiness by achieving external goals, but regardless of whether they achieve these goals or not they realise they still haven't found the happiness they are looking for. This is particularly so because many knights, such as Parcival, sacrifice love and relationships to get external success.

When this happens often enough Knights pass through a kind of depression or Dark Night of the Soul. In the story this is represented by Parzival's horse leading him into the deepest part of the forest.

The Dark Night of the Soul spurs an internal journey of discovery and healing. This often means clearing past parental programming and feelings of inadequacy that they tried to cover up with the pursuit of external success.

Once the Knight has completed this internal journey they find the success, love and happiness they were searching for. It was often right there in front of them all along but their obsession with external results blinded them to its value. It is only after his internal journey that Parcival finds the Grail, becomes a leader in his own right and is reunited with his very patient wife!

This story is so important and the lessons so seminal to a profound understanding of success I have written it in detail with commentary for you at the end of this book. In this way you can gain the benefit of the incredible wisdom encoded in this extraordinary story that has captured our imagination for centuries. The Holy Grail has become a metaphor for achieving our greatest ideals of success, love and happiness.

> ## My Experience
>
> I find setting and achieving goals relatively easy. If I set a goal I am determined to achieve it and I invariably do so unless there is something more important I need to complete instead.
>
> In fact, in the past achieving a goal became a kind of obsession. I would sacrifice my health and my relationships to attain it. Now that I understand The Principles of Achievement more deeply and what success means to me

personally, I set goals with more realistic time frames. This allows me to ensure my business goals are in tune with my lifestyle, health and well-being goals.

For instance I might set a goal that says:

"I am really excited that I have finished my book and it is on or before _____ (specific date), while swimming every second day and happily having the weekends away from my computer with my partner."

What is interesting is that even though I am good at setting and achieving goals I don't find it much fun. I do not feel passionate about this process. When people find a Principle easy to achieve but they don't really feel passionate about it we call this a Talent. Talents are what people are good at and often get paid to do but it doesn't really light them up.

This is different from our Passions. Passions are what we love to do and would want to do even outside of work. Most people have three Passion Principles and one Talent Principle. The talent is the person's strengths. When people marry their passions with their talents they discover their purpose and can make money from what they love. This has been what I have been able to do in my career.

Most people use their talent for work. They are good at it, people appreciate it and they get paid well for it. If people are only doing their talent at work and not their passion as well, they feel uninspired by what they do and it is an effort to stay motivated.

Then a lot of people intuitively discover something they are passionate about so they leave their job and set up their business based on it. When they do this they often don't want to incorporate their talent into their new business because they blame it for why they were unhappy at their old job. Unfortunately for many, they cannot then make money from what they love because the money-making talent principle is missing from their business.

When I work with people in Passion and Purpose Coaching training and individually, I help them discover their passion and how they can combine that with their talent to make a great income from what they love. This stops the seesaw back and forth many people experience between pursuing their passion or making money. Instead with this coaching process it is possible to actually have both.

My own Passion Principles are The Principle of Energy – Innocent Adventurer Archetype, The Principle of Concentration – Magician Archetype and The Principle of Creativity – Creative Nurturer Archetype.

These are The Principles I love to follow. I would be happy to use these Principles on holiday; they energise me and make me feel passionate and happy. I use all three of these Principles in my business to keep me inspired, but if I did not incorporate my Talent Principle of Results – Knight Archetype I would not have a successful business.

Remember, it is the marriage of your passion and your talents that gives you purpose and success.

You may then wonder about the other Principles that do not make up your four. We call these Principles your Challenge Principles and your Invisible Principles. These are areas of challenge or weakness. Working on these Principles will create the greatest transformation and growth for you. In your business or career it is important to play to your strengths in order to be successful and happy. Your strengths are your passions and talent.

## Your Turn

Now that we are at the final step in achievement, taking action and getting successful results, let's summarise how the first 8 Principles of Success work together.

Below I have given you two examples that you can apply in your own life. The first is a business example for the creation of a product or service. The second is an example of finding your love partner. In the end, whatever it is you want to achieve successfully will be exactly the same pattern.

## Business Example

**Step 1** – Be inspired and gain the energy and ideas you need to begin. Brainstorm the product or services you have ideas about. Pick the best and focus on that.

**Step 2** – Concentrate that energy by focusing on what you want.

**Step 3** – Be open and vulnerable and willing to receive. That may be from your own unconscious mind, from research or advice from reputable and qualified sources. Also clear away any negative beliefs, sabotage or blockage.

**Step 4** – Imagine what you want and what it will look like. Create it and nurture it into being. This may be a business, product, service, career path or something else you desire. If it is someone else's product you want to sell, create a way to market it. If you have learnt something and have permission to teach it, ensure you have created your own flavour or style.

**Step 5** – Look at what you have created through the eyes of reason and make sure it has a logical order and structure that others can understand. Make sure you also systematise the delivery of your product or service.

**Step 6** – Let your work sit for a while. Go for a walk, have a weekend off and allow your intuition to speak to you. Look at your product or service again to see if you have any added flashes of intuition to contribute.

**Step 7** – Discern what to keep and what to cut away. Is there waffle in what you have put together? Editing anything extraneous gives what you present more power. Present your product to people you trust who will be supportive and give constructive feedback.

**Step 8** – Take action and put your product or service into the public arena. This includes marketing, sales and business structures that take your product or service to the world.

So now that we are at the final step in achievement, let's summarise how the first 8 Principles work together in finding a long-term love partner.

## Finding a Long-Term Love Partner Example

**Step 1** – Be re-inspired by love and the idea of a relationship. Realise you can start with a clean slate and be enthusiastic about the idea. You might chat to people you know who have great relationships about how they met.

**Step 2** – Focus on the qualities you want in a relationship. Do NOT write a list of what the person should look like or their career. This will train the RAS to focus on fulfilling your list of physical attributes instead of finding the person you relate best with. It may even mean you miss the perfect person because of arbitrary externals like hair colour.

Instead, write down the *qualities* you want in a relationship. For example, it might be sharing love and affection, great communication, listening and understanding, mutual attraction and a wonderful love life. Brainstorm as many as you can think of and order them, from 1 to 10, with number one being the most important.

**Step 3** – Be open and vulnerable and willing to receive. Let people know you are looking for a relationship. Go to a good coach who can help you heal past relationship issues and hurts. Make sure they use a process that allows you to delve into the unconscious mind to clear emotions, beliefs, influences and programming at a deep level. I would of course suggest a coach who was trained in my Matrix Therapies® and Archetypal Coaching®.

**Step 4** – Imagine what it will be like for you to be in a great relationship. Create a concept of what you would do and how you would be in a relationship. Would you like to travel together, share personal development courses together or indulge other interests?

Create time to nurture yourself instead of giving too much to friends and family. Make sure you eat well, look after your health and relax. Have massages and facials, get your hair done, pamper yourself, take yourself on holidays and enjoy being in nature. This self-nurturing will give you a glow that is luminous and attractive.

**Step 5** – Look logically at the types of places where you may meet someone who is suitable for you. This could be through family and friends, or dare I say it, the internet and dating agencies. It might also be found in doing things you enjoy.

Make sure you can establish boundaries so that you can reject people you do not want to be with. It is amazing how many people I know found their love partner after they rejected someone who was not right for them.

**Step 6** – Follow your intuition. Go places and do things because you feel drawn to them. Let intuition guide you instead of fear. Meditate on the type of relationship you want and ask to be guided to the right person. Then surrender to universal timing. Use your intuition to see if there are remaining negative beliefs, blocks or influences that need clearing. I find Passion and Purpose™ Coaching very useful for flushing these out and resolving them.

**Step 7** – Be discerning about who you want to spend your time with but at the same time make sure you are giving people a chance. Trust yourself to know who is right for you but discern that it is intuition driving you and not fear of being hurt.

Make decisions on the basis of self-love rather than worrying about hurting the other person. Remember, if you are continuing to date someone because you don't know how to reject them, then in the long run you are simply wasting their time and your own.

At the end of a date if you are sure this person is not for you say something like:

"You are a fantastic person and I have really enjoyed spending time with you. However, I am looking for my lifelong partner and I don't feel that kind of connection. I wish you all the very best with your search."

If you do like someone let them know you want to take things slowly and get to know them before jumping into a sexual relationship. If you are looking for a long-term partner this is self-loving behaviour. It shows you respect and value yourself enough to give yourself the gift of time.

**Step 8** – Continue to make yourself available and take action until you find someone. Sometimes that will mean giving yourself a break and assessing if your actions are working. Ask yourself if what you are doing is allowing you to meet people with potential. If it is not, take time to find different actions to take.

Sometimes indirect action is useful, such as pursuing a hobby you love or a course you feel passionate about that gets you out. Even starting a business you feel passionate about and attending networking and business functions can open up a new world of potential partners who you would not meet if you kept doing the job you dislike.

Take action to become the person who can have the kind of relationship you are looking for. So take action to develop your confidence and be passionate about life. This creates charisma and internal calm that is very magnetic.

Even with all this action you may find a relationship comes from a completely different source, but the action suggests to yourself and others that this is something you want and are committed to getting.

## The Principle of Results applied to gaining Achievement, Love and Happiness

I had a client who was in his late 50s, he had a stable business that was making good money but he had a goal to increase the business's turnover so he could sell it for a handsome profit. This would further fund his retirement.

The only problem was the goal was taking up so much of his headspace he wasn't taking any time off work. He brought work home at night, he worked over the weekends and he hadn't taken a holiday in years.

He was not making any time to exercise, his diet was unhealthy and he was not spending any quality time with his wife. This meant his intimacy was greatly affected because, like many women, she didn't want to make love simply as a form of stress relief for him. She would prefer to spend quality time together that then led to a romantic night.

His stress level was so high it was affecting his sleep, his motivation and his mood. He had become prone to angry outbursts. This meant his staff were afraid of him. In the short term they may have worked harder but in the long term they were taking sick leave and then quitting just when he had them trained up to do the job properly. He would then take their work on board while he found a replacement.

Just as he built the business up something always seemed to go wrong. By the time I met him he was becoming depressed and even having suicidal thoughts. His doctor was recommending various drugs and he had the support of a psychologist but he wanted to get coaching as well.

With the permission and support of his various doctors he came to me for coaching. This man was a typical Knight in Shadow; he felt if he could just achieve his dream then everything would be OK and he could retire happy.

Unfortunately, just like the story of Parzival, the Holy Grail of his goal seemed to be eluding him. The more he went after it the more it seemed just out of his reach. It was becoming a never-ending quest.

As well as this, the way he was going about achieving his results was more likely to lead him to a heart attack than his goal. Even if he did achieve his dream retirement, it was unlikely to be the solution he was looking for, because suddenly he would be doing nothing. People who are workaholics do not tend to do well with sudden retirement. They simply do not know what to do with themselves and health and psychological issues tend to hit them with a vengeance.

The latest research at the Harvard School of Public Health shows that out of 5422 individuals in the study, those who had retired were 40 per cent more likely to have had a heart attack or stroke than those who were still working. The increase was more pronounced during the first year of retirement. Of course we wanted to avoid this and ensure that he could transition into retirement, while still having meaning in his life.

When we looked deeper into his finances it was clear that with his investments he could actually retire immediately. In fact after taxes and other payouts he would have almost the same amount of money if he sold his business straight away instead of in five years' time. This was not my area of expertise but he had an accountancy background. He could do the figures accurately himself, once he was inspired to do so and with a little prompting.

So it was interesting that the achievement of the goal had become a driving force in and of itself, even though the outcome had no real financial benefit. He had been telling himself this was the purpose of all his hard work, when in reality there would be no significant increase in profit. In fact, by investing the money he could have been better off in the long run, by retiring immediately.

Psychologically however achieving the financial goal he had set himself for the business was massively important to him. He also found it incredibly difficult to even contemplate taking any time off, even though he could see that most of the day he was unproductive and that his moodiness was affecting staff turnover.

When we see a mismatch between the reality of the outcomes of a goal and the desire for the goal we know there is something else driving behaviour. For him this was completely unconscious. There was an unconscious need to be a workaholic and achieve the goal that was different from the financial purpose of the goal. The other interesting point of note was that his moodiness was actually sabotaging all the things he really wanted, including the success of his business, his lifestyle and his relationship.

When I asked this man about his personal history I discovered his father had been a poor tenant farmer, who was a brutal and violent man. Nothing was ever good enough for him. The kids worked long hours after school doing hard manual labour, such as digging holes in hard earth, putting up fences and working with livestock. If they put one foot out of place or didn't work quickly enough they were belted. Sometimes they were hit for no apparent reason. If they did something outstanding, their achievement was always criticised or belittled. It was impossible to please his father.

When my client turned 17 he left home. He put himself through the remainder of his schooling and university. He did white collar work and in his early 20s set up his own business. He never saw his father again but somewhere hidden in his psyche he still wanted to impress his father and was afraid of the consequences of not.

So he worked the same long hours he worked on the farm and never rested. He was afraid of not working because a part of him was still looking over his shoulder expecting the strap. He treated his staff in a similar way to how he had been treated. He was never violent but he was moody, angry and critical.

He worked as if he was a pauper and would starve if he stopped, which had been the reality for his father but far from his own. This part of him was afraid of attaining the goal and retiring because he feared the consequences of not working. At the same time another part of his psyche hated himself for being like his dad and felt he was unworthy of success.

We worked on clearing the negative influence of his father who was, essentially a bully. We also cleared the negative influence of his mother who was a victim who did not stand up for her children. She was also afraid of giving them too much attention or affection in case the father became jealous.

These clearings helped him to stop repeating the same patterns of his father and feel empowered rather than a victim, like his mother. This gave him access to new and more effective behaviours in his own life and in his relationships. He was able to take time off during the weekends, not take work home except during particularly busy periods and take a much-needed holiday.

We looked at which of The 8 Principles of Achievement were his strengths and the corresponding Archetypes. We discovered that the areas of his business he loved was speaking, promotion, the initial sales interview with new clients and follow up progress meetings with existing clients. Everything else he began gradually to delegate. We gave his wife a much more responsible role in the running of the company, in particular management of staff.

This meant he began to enjoy his business more, was less stressed and in the end far more productive. He realised he loved his business and did not want to sell the business in the short term. Instead he could run it from a position of passion rather than desperation. He knew he could sell whenever he chose to.

His mood greatly improved as did his sense of wellbeing. His health and fitness took much longer to achieve and remains a continuing work in progress. His coaching didn't mean he was never down again or that he never had another problem. What it did do was ease his compulsive behaviour so he could make new choices that brought him closer to the purpose of what he really wanted. He could see the goal as a means to an end, not the end itself. He realised he could get self love and self esteem while on the journey. He also understood that this goal was just one of many possible ways he could get what he wanted.

Interestingly, I recently bumped into him three years after our coaching. He had sold his business and was now on the speaking circuit promoting his previous business to new customers. This allowed him to fulfill his Passion and Purpose without the hindrance of all the things he disliked about his old business. It also gives him time off while still having a sense of meaning. It was the perfect combination for him.

Clearing the past opened up new possibilities and choices of behaviour that were previously invisible.

Just like Parzival, this client needed to let go of being fixated on gaining the goal for the goal's sake. His depression actually led him to a desire to make much needed changes. He went through the Dark Night of the Soul and in that dark place he found someone who could assist him to go within. When he cleared the past influences, negative beliefs of unworthiness and negative emotions, he could come out of the 'dark forest' with a new perspective. The Holy Grail was not what he was expecting. His Holy Grail was actually a whole new approach to his life, his business, his goals and his relationships.

Sometimes people put a great deal of time and effort into getting something only to turn around and realise that what they thought they wanted didn't give them the feeling they were expecting.

This is because the formula a lot of people believe will make them happy is faulty. Many people see happiness in an 'if-then' structure.

For example, a person's highest value may be spending quality time with their family but they create a structure in their mind that runs:

"If my business is successful then I will spend time with my family."

By the time their business is successful their family have grown up and don't want to give them the time of day, like the Harry Chapin song, *Cat's in the Cradle.*

"When you coming home, dad?" "I don't know when; We'll get together then, son, you know we'll have a good time then."

Of course the father never finds the time and his son grows up just like him. When the father retires the son then doesn't have the time for him.

People often realise too late that you can actually have a successful business and spend time with the family. It does not have to be one or the other and that sacrificing one for the other simply isn't worth it, both personally and financially. A lot of people sacrifice time with the family to make money only to find that their spouse divorces them and takes more than half the money with them.

People have this 'if then' structure in so many areas of life. Here are the common ones I see regarding success:

"If I am successful then I will be happy."
"If I am successful then I will have time to be creative."
"If I am successful then I will be respected."
"If I am successful then I will be special and significant."
"If I am successful then I can relax."
"If I am successful then I can get healthy."

These are all examples of faulty logic and will certainly create unhappiness, dissatisfaction and disappointment because in fact they are all delusional.

Instead people need to ask themselves:

"How can I make sure I am happy while I become even more successful?"
"How can I use my creativity to become even more successful?"
"How can I be respected while I become even more successful?"
"How can I use my specialness and significance to become even more successful?"
"How can I find time to relax while I become even more successful?"

**SECTION 2**

# Understanding your Journey to Successful Achievement

THE 8 PRINCIPLES OF ACHIEVEMENT, LOVE
AND HAPPINESS – 4 STAGES OF GROWTH
AND THE HERO'S JOURNEY

# FOUR STAGES OF Growth

## Hero's Journey

Adapted from Joseph Campbell with
Archetypal Stages of Growth by Pip McKay

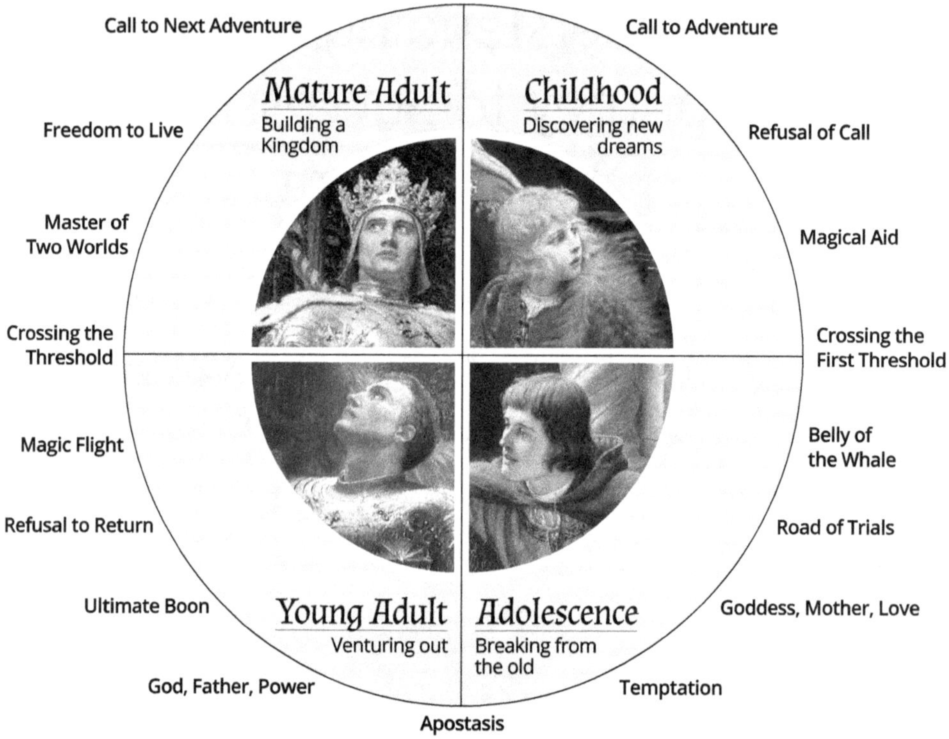

**Mature Adult** — Building a Kingdom
- Call to Next Adventure
- Freedom to Live
- Master of Two Worlds
- Crossing the Threshold
- Magic Flight
- Refusal to Return
- Ultimate Boon

**Childhood** — Discovering new dreams
- Call to Adventure
- Refusal of Call
- Magical Aid
- Crossing the First Threshold
- Belly of the Whale
- Road of Trials
- Goddess, Mother, Love

**Young Adult** — Venturing out
- God, Father, Power

**Adolescence** — Breaking from the old
- Temptation

Apostasis

# FOUR STAGES OF GROWTH

Many people think of progress as a linear advancement like climbing up a mountain, however when we think of success in this way there is nothing to do once we are at the top but to come back down and find another mountain to climb. What happens if we have already climbed the biggest mountain? There is nothing more to achieve.

If instead we think of achievement as a cycle where we learn and gain an ever-greater understanding of ourselves and the world around us then our progress is continuous. Yes, we may begin another cycle but it is a constant spiral up. This progress is not stopped by age or results – it is a constant evolution.

The wonderful thing is that this cycle follows a specific pattern, which we can understand and predict. At each point of the journey there are specific challenges and rewards that further our growth.

When we embark on a quest for success, we actually begin a cycle called the Hero's Journey. The Hero's Journey outlines the steps you take from being an ordinary person having a mundane existence to becoming an extraordinary person who influences others. It is the ultimate leadership development tool, whether that is the leader of a big corporation or the leader of your family and yourself.

Joseph Campbell did pioneering and extraordinary work outlining the structure of the Hero's Journey in his seminal book, *The Hero With a Thousand Faces*, first published in 1949. He studied hundreds of stories, myths and legends from cultures around the world and discovered there really was only one story.

This archetypal story he called the Monomyth, which outlined the journey an ordinary person embarked on to become a Hero. What he discovered was that the steps a Hero takes are always the same. He outlined each one with examples of stories from many different cultures.

With these steps any writer had a blueprint for the structure of a riveting story and it made story writing much easier. The blockbuster movie *Star Wars* followed this structure and had unprecedented success. In the 1990s, a scriptwriter from Disney, called Christopher Vogler, wrote a now legendary memo which outlined these steps of the Hero's Journey in *Star Wars* as a practical tool for scriptwriters.

He suggested all scriptwriters should follow the Hero's Journey. He went on to write the *Lion King*, so he was certainly on to something special. Since then all blockbuster movies have followed this formula. Of course their success also depends on the writer's ability to develop characters and the quality of the acting and direction, among other things, but here at least was the foundation of a successful movie.

When I first found out about the Hero's Journey I was astounded, it was like a veil was lifted. I had always loved stories since I was a child. I felt intuitively drawn to them and knew they had hidden messages encoded in them but I just couldn't find the key. I also felt they had a familiar and repetitive structure but I was always so involved in the storyline and characters I just couldn't see it.

The Hero's Journey revealed the structure to me and that was one incredible key that I really loved. It allowed me to create and tell my own stories more effectively.

It began to occur to me that The 8 Principles were actually a part of the Hero's Journey. Each Principle assisted the Hero at a different stage of his journey. In fact without mastering each Principle the Hero simply could not progress. It was when I discovered this link that I was able to truly decode the metaphoric meaning of stories, myths and legends and I found this incredibly enlightening.

The 8 Principles of Achievement helped me elucidate exactly why each step was important to the Hero's Journey and the precise meanings behind it. The Principles tell us exactly what is happening to the Hero and what qualities he needs to attain in order to be successful.

I have spent a great deal of time and energy studying and understanding the links between these two bodies of work and I have found it truly extraordinary. Through this study I created a new model called Archetypal Stages of Growth. It gives us an easy and incredibly profound system that helps us understand exactly what we need to do and who we need to become to move from living a mundane existence to creating an extraordinary life. It also gives us incredible insights into understanding other people's behaviour and how we can most effectively assist them.

Archetypal Stages of Growth divides the Hero's Journey into four stages of maturation; Childhood, Adolescence, Young Adult and Mature Adult. These are metaphoric stages. Even though the Hero may be an adult when they start a journey they are metaphorically a child; when they go through Tests and Trials they are an adolescent; when they achieve success they are a young adult and when they contribute what they have learnt to others they are a mature adult.

What is interesting for all of us is that even though we may be adults, often parts of our psyche are stuck in the Childhood and Adolescent Stages of Growth. This is the cause of all our reactivity and aberrant behaviour. The ordinary person allows these immature parts of their psyche to rule their lives and their success is sabotaged.

This is because the immature parts of us want the safety of belonging to a pack and at the same time want to feel special at the expense of others. This creates an internal conflict between the child inside who wants to gain love by belonging and therefore doesn't want to do anything different or stand out, and the adolescence inside us who wants to feel significant and unique by competing with their metaphoric siblings for attention. Neither of these two strategies lends itself to effective leadership and the internal conflict between them creates constant drama in people's lives that stops them achieving anything truly worthwhile.

The Hero instead goes on a journey to psychological maturity. This allows the person to become a young adult and achieve success in their own right, which is dependent on them living their unique Passion and Purpose and not on competing with or rebelling against others. Once they have accomplished this, the next stage is to become a mature adult and contribute something worthwhile to others.

The Archetypal Stages of Growth is a fantastic stand-alone model that can be used in transformational coaching work and in all personal and professional development. In fact every stage is essential for maturity. Many people want to skip from Childhood to Young Adult but the fact is, no matter how uncomfortable Adolescence is and how people would like to avoid Tests and Trials, it is an essential stage of growth. We need Adolescence and Tests and Trials to gain the resources we require to achieve our goals. We also need to rebel against old beliefs and programs that have held us back in order to grow.

In reality, Adolescence gives us the strength to leave the nest of our parents' protection and forge our own path. In fact rebellion is an essential step towards independence. It becomes a problem when people are psychologically stuck there and cannot move forward into the next stage of their growth. All Adolescent behaviour is a rebellion against the power of parents on our behaviour because at that time we live at home under their roof and rules. Not wanting to obey others' rules becomes a motivational factor to leave the security of home and become independent.

Many children in this day and age have very few rules at home to rebel against and so simply live with their parents long after they should have left home. This actually hampers the development of their maturity and creates co-dependence with their parents. The child fundamentally never grows up and therefore does not gain both the independence and the responsibility, which is essential for growth.

While this is true in reality with parents and children, it can also be true metaphorically; some people continue to live their life by their parents' rules even though these do not assist them in getting what they really want. I always say to people, "Look at your parents, even if they are nice people, do you want the life, relationships and money that they had?"

If you don't there comes a point where you need to rebel against their beliefs and behaviours in these areas in order to become truly independent.

Once you have rebelled and become independent then it is time to stop looking over your shoulder to ensure you are different from your parents and instead follow your Passion and Purpose in all areas of you life. In this Young Adult Stage of Growth you no longer need to rebel because your parental programming no longer influences you and you are really free to do what you want and be who you are. Along with this freedom however comes the responsibility of looking after yourself. Without having this responsibility you can never be truly free.

In the Mature Adult Stage of Growth your responsibility stops being just to yourself and your Passion and Purpose. In this final stage you are also responsible for contributing to others, making the world a better place or at least your immediate community and creating a lasting legacy.

It is important to understand that until you have cycled through at least one Hero's Journey for yourself you won't be an inspiring influence for others. People look for mentoring from others who have achieved results they want for themselves.

Archetypal Stages of Growth, the Hero's Journey and the Principles of Achievement give us all the tools we need to truly fulfill our potential and become a leader in our own right. They are the keys to becoming a person of influence.

Let's now look at an outline of the Archetypal Stages of Growth and the Hero's Journey and how they link to the 8 Principles of Achievement.

**STAGE 1**

# CHILDHOOD – THE HERO'S JOURNEY BEGINS

When the Hero begins their journey they are in the Childhood stage of growth because they are taking their first steps to becoming a Hero. This is where the potential Hero is asked to step out of the ordinary world and their comfort zone and embark on their journey to become an extraordinary human being.

There are four steps to this stage; the Call to Adventure, the Refusal of the Call, Magical Aid and Crossing the First Threshold. The Childhood Stage of Growth requires the understanding and application of two of the 8 Principles of Achievement.

## Stage 1, Step 1 – The Call to Adventure
### uses the Principle of Energy and the Secret of Inspiration

To take these first steps it is essential you have the first Principle of Achievement, which is Energy, and the corresponding Secret of Inspiration.

Without inspiration you do not have the spark of energy to begin. With inspiration you gain the desire, motivation and the will to initiate action. Think of a time when you heard an outstanding speaker or read a book that inspired you. Did you then feel motivated to take action you would not normally take? Did you make a decision that could potentially change your life?

With inspiration you have the energy to begin your journey towards successful attainment. At this point in the journey the person is the

Archetypal Innocent Adventurer, because the Hero is innocent and does not have experience yet. That innocence is essential. Have you ever heard someone say: "If I had known what it was going to take to start a business, I would have never started, but I am so happy I did." We need that naïvety to just 'go for it'. Innocence provides the enthusiasm, excitement and heightened drive needed to overcome inertia and move forward.

This is not the time to be told about everything that could go wrong; this is the time to feel excited and have a vision of what could go right. There will be time later on to do due diligence and take precautions if necessary, but right at this moment you need to jump off the metaphoric cliff and begin.

## Stage 1, Step 2 – Refusal of the Call

Then comes the Refusal of the Call, which is where you hit the fear barrier. It is where you have doubt. It is all your limiting beliefs, such as: "Who am I to do this?" "What if it doesn't work," "What if people laugh at my ideas," "I am not good enough" and so on. It is these fears that stop ordinary people from moving forward. Everyone has these types of thoughts, it is just that heroes don't let their fears stop them.

If you believe your doubt, it is like the Monopoly board game when you: "Go (back) to jail…do not pass Go." Or as they said in *The Matrix*: "You take the blue pill— the story ends, you wake up in your bed and believe whatever you want to believe."

Ordinary people are victims of their doubt, their circumstances, their parental programming and their fears. These rule the ordinary person's life and keep them stuck.

The Hero has exactly the same issues to overcome but they take the risk, they dare to be different, they deal with their doubts, fears and past experiences. This is not easy; if it were easy you wouldn't become a Hero by doing it.

As Morpheus says later in *The Matrix*: "You take the *red* pill—you stay in Wonderland, and I show you how deep the rabbit hole goes. Remember: all I'm offering is the truth. Nothing more."

He doesn't say he is offering Neo an easy ride, he just says he is offering him the truth and a choice. The decision is up to him. Of course Neo takes the red pill but he could have just as easily taken the blue pill and then there wouldn't be a movie about him! He would be in the movie theatre watching someone else be the Hero and wondering how they built up the courage that he could not.

## Stage 1, Step 3 – Magical Aid
### uses the Principal of Concentration and the Secret of Focus

So how does the Hero overcome their fears, limiting beliefs and doubts?

Well, usually the Hero has some help. A wise person, or mentor, who helps the Hero transform their fears into a decision to change. It is important to understand that the wise one cannot make the decision for the Hero but they can help the Hero see their choices or loosen the grip of fear.

In coaching we would use a process like Matrix Therapies® to help the person overcome parental programming, fears and doubts to assist the client to make change. In the end the individual has to make the decision themselves to begin that journey. After all, you can't coach someone who doesn't turn up or doesn't want to participate in the process. The Hero has to want to change and take action, even if at first there is a little resistance.

This wise person is often referred to as the Magician or similar title in the Hero's Journey. They have the capacity to help the Hero focus on what they want and clarify options just as Morpheus does in the quote above. Through that concentration the real Hero is able to make a decision and cross the first threshold into the next stage of growth that I have labelled Adolescence.

**STAGE 2**

# ADOLESCENCE – CROSSING THE FIRST THRESHOLD

This is where the Hero experiences all the Tests and Trials that make them mature. The Hero needs these Tests and Trials in order to grow, learn and gain resources. They need to rebel against the security of parental programming and old comfort zones in order to step into who they really are and become fully independent.

There are a number of steps in the Adolescence stage of growth. It starts with the Belly of the Whale, then Tests and Trials, Meeting the Goddess, Temptation and finally Apostasis (symbolic death and resurrection). Let's go through them in more detail and The Principles involved to progress to the next stage.

## Stage 2, Step 1 – Belly of the Whale
### uses the Principle of Receptivity and the Secret of Vulnerability

After the exertions of Crossing the First Threshold there is a period of what I call grace, but is officially called The Belly of the Whale. It is almost like those in-between ages of 11 and 12, before adolescence really begins – you're not really a child but you're not a teen either. This gives the Hero the time to rest, recuperate and gather resources for the Tests and Trials ahead.

In *The Matrix* it was when Neo first entered the space ship, the Nebuchadnezzar, and was under the glass dome with all the acupuncture needles in him, restoring his muscle mass. Here he was receiving help and sustenance and he was vulnerable. This was necessary for him to become strong enough to face the challenges to come.

I find this often happens in business. After making the big decision to leave your job and set up a business there is often a quieter preparation time before you make your offering public. It may be when you do a course to learn the skills you need. Or it may be writing the website content and getting help to set it up. At this time there is a certain vulnerability as you do not really know what you are doing and it makes it much easier if you are receptive to learning, advice and assistance.

## Stage 2, Step 2 – Tests and Trials

In stories and movies this is where the majority of action happens. The Hero faces all kinds of challenges that test their resolve and develop their skills. In *The Matrix* this is when Neo develops his fighting skills, fights the agents and discovers more about the Matrix.

There will always be Tests and Trials when we do something different because our body, emotions, mindset and personality have to adjust to who we are becoming. We are breaking out of the old and discovering the new. It is often a time of confusion where you are no longer who you used to be but you have not yet become who you want to be.

You may have experienced this when you received a promotion and all of a sudden you have to deal with managing staff and being responsible for a team's results.

Or perhaps your savings run out and you really have to make a living from your business.

Or maybe you applied some marketing strategies that didn't work or your web designer ran off with your money and your website isn't up.

Or a client is unhappy with your product or service and wants a refund just when your spouse loses their job.

Or you are in a new relationship and suddenly the honeymoon period is over and the teenage son starts living with you both.

# STAGE 2 – ADOLESCENCE – CROSSING THE SECOND THRESHOLD

Or you finally start getting results at the gym and your boss suddenly wants you to work late to finish a large project.

No matter what area of life you make major change in, there will always be a period of time where there are challenges. These Tests and Trials help you see what you are made of, they make you find and develop your inner strength and outer resources. When you understand this, you are emotionally prepared for when they come along. Tests and Trials of some kind are part of the journey. The bigger the change you make and the more different you need to be to sustain those changes, the larger the challenges feel.

For instance, imagine a shy person, whose parents have always lived in the country and had little education. Now imagine that at seventeen this person decided that they wanted to be the first person in the family to go to university in the city. That would be a huge change and the challenges the person would feel would be very different from someone whose family was city-dwelling academics.

In the end it doesn't matter whether the change someone is making would be easy for someone else. What is important is the size of the change for that person and the courage it takes to make it. This is what really determines Hero status. That is why Frodo, in *Lord of the Rings,* is such a great hero because his incredible achievement is so outside of normal Hobbit behaviour.

If it was easy to be the Hero it wouldn't take someone special to make it happen. Just know this is the time when you learn the most but it is imperative that you allow yourself to learn, find solutions and keep moving forward.

Just as Dory sings in *Finding Nemo,* "Just keep swimming! Just keep swimming!"

The great news is that there is a Principle to help you on your way and most people simply don't know it. Without this Principle you just keep hitting your head against a brick wall – with it you are able to problem-solve and innovate.

So what is it?! "Just keep reading! Just keep reading!"

## Stage 2, Step 3 – Meeting the Goddess
### uses the Principle of Creativity and the Secret of Imagination

So what does this mean? Well the fact is that you will never be able to resolve these new Tests and Trials with old thinking.

As Albert Einstein said, "We cannot solve our problems by using the same kind of thinking we used when we created them."

So how do we solve the challenges of Tests and Trials? Well, we have to use our imagination to see different possibilities and then create solutions. This is attributed to Meeting the Goddess because the Goddess is always seen as a creative being because the feminine gives birth. So metaphorically, instead of working harder we need to find more creative ways of working smarter.

The other quality attributed to the Goddess in the Hero's Journey is love. In times of trouble what we really need is love, support and encouragement. We do not need someone telling us off or criticising us. What we need is for someone to listen and understand our frustrations, as well as encourage our new ideas. This, symbolically, is the Goddess. With that assistance we can relax and begin to look outside the box of the problems to where solutions lie.

So when you are going through Tests and Trials find someone who is supportive of you, someone who is on your side and talk to them. Brainstorm ideas without judgment and explore options. Then look at what is most likely to work and apply that. You will find that, with this kind of support, you will come back into the flow.

If you don't have someone external to help you at this moment then make sure you change your mindset from frustration to understanding. Stop bashing yourself up and realise that these challenges will stimulate your growth as you look for solutions. Do not indulge in recriminations for what you did in the past, your problems are there to assist you in developing resources. You become wise by facing and overcoming challenging situations.

## STAGE 2 – ADOLESCENCE – CROSSING THE SECOND THRESHOLD

Remember to be more compassionate with yourself, have a break, eat good food, have a massage and then come back to the problem with fresh eyes. This often makes problems much easier to solve and is more supportive of your journey. In fact the word 'problem' literally means 'to throw forth a question for which you know there is a solution', just like the mathematical problem of $1 + 2 = ?$. The problem is set so we can work out that the solution is 3. Understand that if you can identify the problem, you have the solution waiting in the wings if you take the time to look for it.

In *The Matrix* Neo has Trinity, who is understanding, loving and supportive of what he is going through. Neo also visits the Oracle who is a loving and truth-telling mother figure who helps him see things differently. Usually at this stage of the Hero's Journey we see both the feminine figures of the 'maid' or love interest and the 'mother' that supports the Hero on his quest.

## Stage 2, Step 4 – Temptation

During this time of Tests and Trials the Hero always faces the temptation of giving up. Temptation may come from an external person who exacerbates the Hero's original doubts and fears. It may be a friend or family member who tempts you to take the easy option and give up. Or it may be your own internal sense that it is all simply too hard. What I love about this section in the Hero's Journey is that it lets us all know that heroes have exactly the same temptations as ordinary people; the difference is they do not give into temptation. Instead they find new ways to keep going. The temptation serves to strengthen their resolve.

In life it is important to identify what the journey actually is so that you know what the temptation is. The temptation calls you to repeat old patterns of behaviour, the journey takes you to new stages of development. If you are someone who martyrs yourself to others' needs and neglect your own, then the temptation will be to continue to martyr yourself to an ever greater degree. Do not kid yourself that this makes you a hero. This is simply a repeated pattern of your old behaviour that keeps you stuck and is probably a repeat of parental programming.

Ask yourself, was your mother or father a martyr? Or perhaps they were both self-centred and you compensated for their selfishness by becoming a martyr. Either way you are still reacting to their programming instead of following your own path. An alternative in this scenario is that the Hero learns to say 'No' and create boundaries. This gives you the time and energy to find and fulfil your destiny even in the face of others' demands.

If however you are someone who always fulfills your own needs and finds it hard to have love and connection, then you would embark on the Hero's Journey when you seek a long-term love partner and negotiate your own needs in the face of someone else's. In this case the Hero's actions would be to incorporate the needs of others and find creative win/win solutions rather than rejecting others to ensure their actions are unencumbered.

## Stage 2, Step 5 – Apostasis, Death and Rebirth

This second threshold is seminal. It is called Apostasis, which literally means death and resurrection - the ordinary person dies and the Hero is truly born. Before this the Hero is really an apprentice hero, after Apostasis they are fully fledged.

In a story this process is usually facilitated or reinforced by the Hero facing their biggest challenge. This may happen before, during or after Apostasis and is called meeting God the Father, because the Hero has to face a symbol of authority or control that stands in their way.

At first, the Hero may even seem defeated by this father figure and appear to die, but then they are resurrected as the Hero and are able to defeat the enemy. In this case they meet the father figure before and after Apostasis and the final defeat of the enemy proves their Hero status.

In life this challenge is usually an old way of being or a dysfunctional behaviour that metaphorically dies. For example, perhaps a person is a spendthrift and this negative behaviour means that they spend all their savings. At Apostasis the person is able to defeat this internal demon and become the Hero instead. The spendthrift dies and the Hero can now achieve and sustain their financial goals.

In this example, at the point of Apostasis the person will usually face a very challenging situation that in the past would have meant that they escaped into uncontrollable spending. But now, as the Hero, they face the stressful situation, sort it out and enjoy the security of having savings and building a financial foundation.

Before Apostasis the person may be tested but fail to resist the temptation to spend but this defeat creates the resolve to never do it again. Then after Apostasis they overcome their addiction and they are able to resist temptation even in stressful times.

After Apostasis the Hero crosses the Second Threshold and there is no going back. It is like when someone is truly mature they no longer want to live with their parents any more. If they do, they are actually still psychologically a teenager pretending to be an adult, like a teenager going away on holiday with friends only to return to their parents. However, when someone truly leaves home, they become a Young Adult and have reached a new independent stage of life.

Even though we have mentioned meeting the father figure in this section I have reserved more detailed discussion for the next section, as this is when it most commonly occurs in stories and films.

## STAGE 3

# YOUNG ADULT – CROSSING THE SECOND THRESHOLD

It is by facing their fear that the Hero crosses the Second Threshold and becomes the Young Adult. This also prepares the Hero to get what they really want. To achieve their ultimate goal the Hero must become the person who can reach it, receive it and appreciate it. This is what all the Tests and Trials have prepared the Hero for; to become the person who fulfills the goal.

When we go through a lot to achieve our goal we appreciate it more. In business you appreciate more what you have worked a great deal to get. It is human nature to respect what has taken much effort to achieve. Once effort has been put in however you are grateful for the ease and grace that comes with flow. If things have always been given to you easily they are rarely respected. This is why so often the grandchild of a self-made multimillionaire loses or spends all the money because they just don't appreciate it. The self-made multimillionaire puts in all the work and knows what it takes; the second generation saw their parent hard at work and often had to sacrifice time with their parent so they appreciate the effort, but the grandchild often has no appreciation whatsoever.

This is not just in business and money. I know in my own life that if I had not had the negative relationships I had before meeting my fiancé, I would not appreciate him in the way I do now.

People see others' achievements but usually do not see the time, energy and effort the person put in. To get what you want requires an investment, but so does doing a job you don't like. As Jim Carey said:

# STAGE 3 – YOUNG ADULT – CROSSING THE SECOND THRESHOLD

"You can fail at what you don't want so you might as well take a risk on what you love."

To achieve there is always a price to pay and you need to be willing to make the investment. However, there is also a price to pay for not achieving what you want. It is important to think about which investment will give you the most return.

## Stage 3, Step 1 – God the Father
### uses the Principle of Organisation and the Secret of Insight

As mentioned before most often it is after Apostasis that the Hero faces their biggest challenge, and it is usually with someone who is like a dark father figure. So this stage is called Meeting God the Father. It is as if the Hero's rebirth needs to have a final test in order to ensure it is complete. In *The Matrix*, Neo fights Agent Smith before Apostasis and Neo appears to die only to be reborn as The One. He then needs to immediately fight Agent Smith again but this time with his new powers he is successful.

Prior to Apostasis Agent Smith appeared invincible; afterwards he is nothing. It is by facing this nemesis, or enemy, that the Hero learns about their own transformation. Sometimes this figure threatens someone or something the Hero loves and this brings out a greater, more mature aspect of their personality.

Usually this authority figure has some kind of organisation behind him. This old order needs to be broken down by the Hero so that a new order can begin, based on the light rather than dark. Organisation and order is important, it is just whether that structure represses people or creates a safe environment to support expression and creativity. After all, you cannot have a thriving economy in a country that has civil war. There are so many countries rich in resources but poor because of conflict.

It is incredibly important the Hero is not just a destroyer of the old but can also inspire or create a new and different form of organisation. In this way the Hero becomes the author in his own life and therefore his own authority. With this new authority however comes responsibility for self and later, in the Mature Adult phase, responsibility for others. The Hero can no longer blame someone else for their circumstances but has to become responsible for their own results. They also have no need to rebel any more because they are the creative force and the ruler in their own life.

In business this shadow father figure could be a large competitor stealing your Intellectual Property or a co-worker bullying you. It could be a recession or a takeover by a major company – whatever is the biggest challenge you have to face and overcome. Sometimes you have to create a boundary or take legal action. Sometimes they have to report behaviour to a greater authority or have a very challenging conversation where you assert yourself. Whatever it is, it will be the thing you have avoided in the past. By facing these challenges you truly transform and move into who you will become – you become the Hero in your own life.

You know the saying: "What doesn't destroy you makes you stronger." This refers to this part of the journey.

The Principle of Organisation may seem odd in these circumstances but the fact is we have to break down the old way we organised our lives and create a new empowering order. The Secret of Insight allows a person to see what is really going on and take wise action. Insight allows us to see what we are really made of and know that all those fears are actually irrational. If we step into our own power the fears melt away. If the fears are real then we need to have all the courage of the Hero to face them and not run away. To step into that power we have to be able to see it within ourselves. Standing up, asserting and speaking our truth are all essential qualities and are the outcome of real insight.

Sometimes with insight we realise that we actually have to walk away. If you are someone who normally confronts then walking away may be a heroic action for you. But if you are someone who normally walks away then standing firm is the heroic action. With insight we can see our actions within the greater context of our normal behaviour. If we want to have an outcome that is different from our old frustrations and disempowerment, then we need to take new action that maybe uncomfortable for us. It is not the action itself that determines whether or not we are the Hero but whether that action takes us in a new direction that is different from our old repeated patterns of behaviour.

## Stage 3, Step 2 – Achieving the Ultimate Boon (Prize)

### uses the Principle of Intuition and the Secret of Listening

In the Young Adult phase the Hero achieves the Boon, which is basically the thing they are really looking for, their ultimate goal. In *The Matrix* it is where NEO discovers he is really the ONE, which is of course a rearrangement of his name, Neo. He has always been the One, he just confused the letters!

The Boon could be winning a trophy, being awarded Business Person of the Year, your book hitting the best-seller list, buying your dream house, finding a health solution that works or your ultimate love partner. It is what you have been searching for and your Tests and Trials have prepared you to find.

Sometimes the Ultimate Boon is not what we thought we wanted but rather what we really want. In *Gone with the Wind*, Scarlett O'Hara thought she loved Ashley Wilkes, only to realise the she really loved Rhett Butler, the man in front of her who had supported her all along.

One of the hidden aspects of Achieving the Boon is that there is a moment of intense intuition just before attaining the prize that allows the Hero to be successful. The Hero has to listen to their inner tuition, their inner self, their internal guidance system in order to achieve the Boon and be successful. This allows them to make the right decisions. They no longer rely on their external mentor or teacher, instead they access their own internal wisdom and become certain about the right action to take.

They stop being reactive to their environment and can listen to and respond from an internal knowing. We see this in *The Matrix* when

Neo realises he is The One during his battle with Smith. He accesses a knowing deep within that allows him to see the true nature of the Matrix and respond appropriately.

In business and life this is where everything comes into flow and you are able to access your genius, and therefore get the results you have been searching for. Often at this moment others sense there is something special about you and want to reward, acknowledge and respect you.

This flow could not happen however without the Tests and Trials earlier in the Adolescence Stage. These clear and widen the channel through which flow can happen. It is through overcoming the Tests and Trials that the Hero gains the confidence and self-esteem to trust themselves and therefore achieve the Ultimate Boon.

## Stage 3, Step 3 – Refusal of Return

It is now time for the Hero to return to the ordinary world and bring their boon, or prize, back to assist others. If you have ever engaged in a personal development course this is the time you go back home and share your new knowledge or your new way of being with others.

The Hero can have a moment where they don't want to go back home because they know they will now have to think of others as well as themselves. They are also aware that others may not like their new way of being and they may not find it easy to fit in because they are now different. We see this with Frodo in *Lord of the Rings*; his journey has changed him and he knows he will no longer really belong at Bag End in the Shire.

## Stage 3, Step 4 – Magical Flight

The Hero eventually makes the journey home and this is called the Magical Flight. In the film *The Matrix* he really does fly like superman back to the city. In *Lord of the Rings*, Frodo flies home on a giant eagle. For many of us who have travelled overseas, coming home may also literally entail a flight but usually this is a metaphorical concept of returning home or back to ordinary life after the journey of transformation.

## STAGE 4

# MATURE ADULT – CROSSING THE THIRD THRESHOLD

So, finally the Hero crosses the Third Threshold and returns to ordinary life. The Hero has now become the Mature Adult, with all its responsibilities and fulfillment.

### Stage 4, Step 1 – Master of Two Worlds
### uses the Principle of Discernment and the Secret of Self-Love

Now that the Hero has come home they can consolidate all the lessons they have learnt and contribute something incredibly worthwhile and special to others. They can help others become heroes too by their example or mentorship. It is here they transform into a leader. They become the person who influences others rather than the person who is being influenced by others. This is particularly important as they return to their old environment. They need to ensure they are the Influencer rather than the Influenced. This guarantees that they do not return to their old ways of being but rather continue their new level of evolution.

The best way to do this is to lead by example. Show others how much richer and more fulfilled you are now you have learnt this new information or made these changes. Many people at this stage become evangelical and try to force others to see their point of view. This type of approach is not usually as effective as allowing others to see your change and then ask you what you have done.

The Principle of Discernment is absolutely key in this Mature Adult stage. True maturity requires the ability to know what to keep and what to cut away. The discerning adult knows when to speak and assist someone and when to remain quiet so that they can learn from their own mistakes and actions.

The mature adult loves themselves enough to avoid making reactive decisions that are the result of seeking attention and approval. They know their own value and can stay or walk away depending on what is needed for the highest good. They can also find a balance between their own needs and those of others, finding creative win-win solutions. They have true self-esteem and self-respect.

The Master of Two Worlds is able to bring and contribute what they learnt on their journey and apply it to the ordinary world to make it extraordinary as well.

## Stage 4, Step 2 – Freedom to Live
### uses the Principle of Results and the Secret of Action

The Hero now has the Freedom to Live in a way that truly reflects who they have become. They take action that is the expression of their highest potential while accessing their genius and inspiring others. Their results are in tune with their Passion and Purpose and are for the highest good of all involved and the greater society. They do not martyr themselves to assist others nor do they get what they want at the detriment of others. They are free to be themselves and others are free to be themselves around them. Their mature freedom allows them to fulfil their potential, follow thier passion and purpose and be a shining example to others to do the same.

## Stage 4, Step 3 – Call to the Next Adventuer
### uses the Principle of Energy and the Secret of Inspiration again

Does it end? Well, yes for that particular cycle. Then, after enjoying the fruits of your labour, it is time to begin again and start a new adventure

## STAGE 4 – MATURE ADULT – CROSSING THE THIRD THRESHOLD

with something else. It is a continuous upward spiral of evolution rather than a repeated pattern that gets you down.

Someone who is successful in business but ignored their love life might start a new adventure by entering into a relationship.

So the journey of improvement continues to greater levels of achievement and fulfillment. Where does it end? Who knows, perhaps never or perhaps we eventually reach some form of enlightenment – but that is the subject of another book. For now it's about learning the 8 Principles of Achievement that allow us to be successful while also finding love and happiness.

In the final section of this book we will revisit the Hero's Journey and the accompanying Principles by looking at one of the world's most enduring and inspiring quest legends, Parzival and the Holy Grail. After all, in the end, we all want to find that elusive Holy Grail of Success whatever that means to us.

**SECTION 3**

# Archetypal Story of the Hero's Journey to the Ultimate Achievement

### PARZIVAL AND THE
### QUEST FOR THE HOLY GRAIL

*A Journey through all the Archetypal Stages of Growth and*
*The 8 Principles of Achievement, Love and Happiness*
*From Innocent Adventurer to Successful Knight*

# PARZIVAL AND THE Holy Grail

# PARZIVAL AND THE HOLY GRAIL

A Retelling by Pip McKay
– based on 'Parzival and the Stone from Heaven –
A Grail Romance Retold for Our Time' by Lindsay Clarke

This final section is the story of Parzival and his quest for the Holy Grail. It is designed to embed into the subconscious mind all the previous learnings from *The 8 Principles of Achievement, Love and Happiness*. It will also give you an archetypal example of how the Hero goes through the Archetypal Stages of Growth and what Principles he uses to assist him on that journey. Stories have been used for thousands of years to make information more memorable and accessible. They also appeal to more 'right brain learners' and make the information more interesting and fun. There is a profound understanding and depth of wisdom that can only be realised when we access the mythic.

As you read the story you will see that I have described what is happening in each part of the Hero's Journey in italics. If you want to engage with the story on its own first simply skip over the sections in italics. Then you can revisit those sections to gain more conscious knowledge. It may help to then revisit the previous chapters of the book, to gain a deeper understanding of each Principle.

**STAGE 1**

# CHILDHOOD – THE HERO'S JOURNEY BEGINS

*(At this point in time Parzival is completely naïve. Like a baby he has no idea who he is. In medieval literature this type of character was often called a Natural or Holy Fool. There is a kind of divine grace in his innocence but no wisdom, understanding or power.)*

Once upon a time there was a young man who did not know who he was, he did not know where he was from, he did not even know his name.

He had seen no other person his whole life except his mother and they had lived alone in the forest.

In fact he thought his name was 'Dear Heart', for that is what his mother called him.

Her name was Herzeloyde and she had been a Queen, but her father, her husband and her two older sons had died in battle as knights.

In her grief she reasoned that if her youngest son was never a knight then he would never die fighting.

She alone would keep him safe from such a destiny.

So in the middle of the night she stole him away into the deep, dark forest and brought him up as innocent as a fawn. As he grew up she continually advised him: "Always follow God's light", hoping this would keep him out of harm's way.

One day, while he was out hunting with his javelin, he heard a great thunderous disturbance in the forest.

Suddenly, there broke from the trees a violence of white light.

The light jarred and shimmered and before his eyes transformed into three huge men, mounted on monstrous horses, galloping towards him.

He was so dazzled that he fell to his knees and opened his arms wide.

"Art thou God?" he cried.

The three knights (as that is what they were) reined in their horses.

The light was simply the sun's dazzling rays, reflecting off their armour.

"Whoa Gringolet!" cried the leader, before his spirited horse trampled the boy to the ground.

"Art thou God?" the boy repeated as he stared into the knight's amused face. "My mother told me, 'always follow God's light.'"

"No fool," said the burly knight at the leader's side, "that is Gawain, although some women think he is God's Gift!"

"If you are not God, what art thou then?" whispered the boy in rapt awe.

"Why Sir Innocence," said Gawain. "We are knights! Now you must let us pass."

Instead the boy grasped Gawain's bridle: "A knight? I do not know what a knight is but you are more beautiful than God. Make me a knight too, so I can be as you are."

"Only High King Arthur at Caerleon can make you a knight, but you must prove yourself worthy of that honour. Now unhand my horse, boy, we must be on our way."

With that Gawain pushed the boy out of the way and the three knights galloped away.

The boy raced home. "Mother, mother I know my destiny, I know what I want to do with my life!" he cried, "I want to follow God's light and become a knight!"

## Stage 1, Step 1 – The Call to Adventure
### Principle of Energy, Secret of Inspiration

*(At this point Parzival becomes the Archetype of the Innocent Adventurer and he is the Principle of Energy. He has become inspired and this gives him the motivation and enthusiasm to want to leave the certainty of home and begin his quest to become a knight)*

Herzeloyde fell to her knees. "No my son you must never be a knight, that way leads only to death and darkness."

"No Mother, I met knights in the wood and they shone brighter than God's Grace. I shall be a knight and nothing, not even you, will stop me," he declared.

Herzeloyde saw that it was hopeless to dissuade him and in her crazed mind realised her only hope was for him to be rejected as unworthy by Arthur's court.

"Well," she said cunningly, "if you wish to be a knight you must have the right clothes."

She searched the lean-to shed where the animals sheltered and found the dirtiest, smelliest sackcloth covered in manure and made a shirt and cowl for her son.

Then she said, "And you must have a horse."

She drew out their old swayed-back nag and put an old blanket on its back.

"Finally, you must have a weapon! Take your javelin with you, Dear Heart, that is an honourable weapon for a knight."

Then she could keep up the charade no longer. "Dear Heart, please do not leave me, you shall die just as your father did. He too was a knight!"

"My father was a knight? Then it must be my destiny to be one!" he declared much to his mother's horror.

To comfort her he said: "Mother, you always told me to follow God's Light and I have seen that light and now I must follow it."

Herzeloyde realised there was nothing more she could do and so in a last attempt to protect her son she said: "Well then my son, heed my advice and do me this last honour."

"Very well, Mother."

"I ask of you only three things.

"You must honour and help all women but as a reward you can ask for no more than a chaste kiss and maybe a ring.

"Never take off these clothes that I have made for you, for they are filled with my love.

"And finally, heed the advice of old men for they have gained the wisdom to grow old."

"Yes mother I will honour your request. Now farewell," and with that the boy impatiently kicked the old horse and was off at a gambolling pace.

The boy travelled day and night through a countryside ravaged by war.

Finally, he came to Caerleon. There he found a Red Knight was haranguing the castle and challenging anyone who dared to come in or out of the gates.

The boy however looked so ridiculous that the Knight let him pass, thinking him unworthy of engagement.

As the boy approached the courtyard a door flew open and a Fool was being tossed out into the dust.

"Don't show your face again until you think of something more amusing," shouted a big, burly knight.

The boy was astonished but soon regained his manners, "God protect you good sir. Can you show me the way to the High King Arthur? I mean to be knighted."

The Fool was about to shoo this mooncalf away when suddenly a thought crossed his mind. Maybe this Natural Fool would make the court laugh and they could forget the troubles the Red Knight had brought.

"Certainly, Sir," cried the Fool, "Come this way!"

The Fool led the boy, still riding his old nag, into the court and announced, "This noble man wishes to be knighted, Sire."

"What's this?" said King Arthur, his mouth twitching with a smile as he looked at the boy, in sackcloth, astride the sway-backed mare.

"It is true, Sir King, make me a knight," declared the boy.

By now the court began to laugh.

Arthur, seeing the boy was in earnest and controlling himself better than most, said: "Boy, to be a knight you must win honours in battle. So you see unless you have done that I can't make you a knight."

## Stage 1, Step 2 – Refusal of the Call

*(The Refusal of the Call can come in many forms; sometimes the potential Hero refuses the call themselves out of fear or reluctance. This is what Neo does in The Matrix. At other times the refusal comes from someone else influential – for Parzival the refusal comes from King Arthur. Then Parzival himself refuses the call after he kills the Red Knight and the Fool suggests he goes back in to court and claim his knighthood.)*

Suddenly, a big, burly knight stood up. "Sire, I know this dolt. We met him in the forest. He is a simpleton!"

Then the knight turned on the boy. "Kill the Red Knight if you want honours, then you can return to the court."

By now the boy felt humiliated. "I shall then," he declared and wheeled his nag around. He left with as much dignity as he could muster, with their laughter ringing in his ears.

When he came outside he felt a fury build inside his guts as he had never felt before.

When he saw the Red Knight he declared, "I challenge you, Sir!"

But the Red Knight replied, "What is this, does Arthur dishonour me so?"

# STAGE 1 – CHILDHOOD – THE HERO'S JOURNEY BEGINS

In that moment the boy saw red and knowing no codes of conduct or chivalry, he picked up his javelin and threw it at the Red Knight.

The Knight did not even have time to pull down his visor before the javelin, pieced him in the eye. He swayed for a moment in his saddle before crashing down off his horse, stone dead.

In amazement the Fool said: "Well Sir Innocent, it looks like you have won your title. Don your new armour and go back inside and claim your knighthood."

"I'll not go back in there to be ridiculed and humiliated," he said, "but I will take the armour and the horse."

The Fool went with the boy to where the Red Knight lay. For a moment the boy was afraid of what he had done. He had never seen a person die before and here he had been the very cause.

But the Fool stripped the body and said, "Now take off those stinky clothes and wear your reward".

"My mother made me these clothes and for love of her I will not part with them."

"Have it your own way then." The Fool helped the boy don his armour over the top of his sackcloth and mount the charger.

Then he farewelled the boy saying, "You may be a natural fool boy, but you have more dignity than half the knights in there. I wish you well".

The boy left without even a glance goodbye. So overwhelmed was he by the turn of events that he wandered off with no idea where he was going.

He let the horse find its own way hoping to escape the humiliation of the court and the horror of his own actions.

Had he really just killed a man, and not just a man but a knight such as his father had been?

As night began to fall, the boy saw an old man. He was well dressed and noble holding a hawk in the middle of the meadow.

"God protect you, good Sir," the boy called out.

"And you too, Sir Knight," the old man replied. "Have you taken a wound?"

"No, Sir," replied the boy.

"Then why do you hold your shield in that manner."

"Because Sir, I have no idea how to hold a shield," replied the boy.

Stunned by this response the old man said, "Maybe you should come with me. Perhaps you are tired and need to rest and then you might have a story to tell me?"

"My mother always told me to take the advice of old men because they had the wisdom to grow old," the boy replied.

Thinking this was an odd response from a knight, the old man asked: "And who was your mother, Sir Knight?"

"Her name is Herzeloyde and I am Dear Heart," he replied.

For a long moment the old man gaped at him in silence, then sank to his knees. "God be praised. I am Gurnemanz, my Lord, and once was marshal to your mother, the Lady Herzeloyde. Your name is not Dear Heart, but Parzival!"

## Stage 1, Step 3 – Magical Aid
### Principal of Concentration, Secret of Focus

*(Parzival meets a wise old man who happens to be his parent's old marshal, called Gurnemanz. The Archetype here is the Magician. This is because Gurnemanz has the capacity and ability to help Parzival transform from a fool into a knight. He does this by focusing Parzival's abundant energy and concentrates the boy's attention on the knowledge and skills he needs to succeed.)*

"Old man, how is this possible and why are you kneeling to me?"

"Do you not know who you are, my Lord?"

The boy shook his head because he was beginning to realise the world was not as it seemed. He indeed did not know who he was or his place in it.

"You, Parzival are the Lord of all this great land. My sons died defending your birthright but all the lands were lost and we could not regain them.

Parzival felt his lungs fill with pride; finally he knew his name and his place. With great dignity he said: "You have had grievous losses, Sir. Your sons cannot be reborn but they can be avenged and land regained."

The old man looked up at Parzival in wonder. But then seeing his sackcloth sticking through his armour and his clumsy seat on his mount, he realised there was much to be done. So he ushered Parzival into his home and began the long task of training him to be a true knight and honour his birthright.

## STAGE 2

# ADOLESCENCE – CROSSING THE FIRST THRESHOLD

*(It is through the help of Gurnemanz that Parzival is able to finally cross the first threshold in his journey to become a knight. Prior to this he has a childlike desire for someone to simply give him a knighthood without him putting in any work to deserve it. This is similar to how a child is provided with food, shelter and clothing without having to do anything to earn the money to buy it. Parzival refuses a knighthood after he kills the Red Knight because he knows he achieved his aim through luck and not through learning the skills he needs to really earn a knighthood. This actually begins the process of his maturity and he crosses the first threshold.)*

### Stage 2, Step 1 – Belly of the Whale
#### Principle of Receptivity, Secret of Vulnerability

*(The Belly of the Whale is a period of grace and rest when the Hero regains his strength after the upheavals of Crossing the First Threshold. Here Parzival is looked after and nurtured and this prepares him for his later Tests and Trials. With Gurnemanz he is able to be vulnerable and receive instruction and guidance because he feels safe from ridicule. He is also aware that he has much to learn in a small amount of time and this is reflected in his desire to ask so many questions. With his mentor he has no concern about appearing ignorant and wants to make up for the time he has spent away from court.)*

Gurnemanz taught Parzival all he knew.

The younger man, conscious of all his lost time, inundated the marshal with question after question.

## STAGE 2 – ADOLESCENCE – CROSSING THE FIRST THRESHOLD

He was tireless in his pursuit of knowledge and quick at arms.

So the months passed. Gurnemanz had never seen a youth so talented, so quick to learn, and have so much dedication as Parzival.

Then there came a day where Parzival had bested every man at arms in Gurnemanz's keep and the marshal had no more answers to give to his questions.

At dinner the old man said, "Parzival I have nothing more to teach you, but you are like a son to me. I thought, perhaps you would like to stay and marry my daughter."

"Dear father, for that is how I think of you, your daughter is beautiful but like a sister to me, as I am like a brother to her. I know my destiny lies elsewhere. However, I do have one more question for you."

"Oh Parzival stop with the questions! If you wish to go out into the world you must remember that a wise knight never reveals his ignorance. So practice now and stop asking so many questions!" the old man exclaimed, in mock frustration.

"As you say father, but this is one question I must ask."

"Very well, go ahead."

"Am I ready? Am I worthy of being a knight?"

"Ahh," the old man exhaled. "Yes Parzival, you are worthy."

"Then, although it grieves my heart to leave you, tomorrow I must go and seek adventure in the wide world."

"Very well Parzival, it is time. I will not try to keep you here as your mother kept you in the forest. It is time for you to go out into the world and truly become a man."

The next day with sadness and great affection Parzival farewelled the family he had grown to love and left the comforts of his newfound home to explore the world.

The moment he left the gates his spirits soared with a sense of excitement and anticipation, such as he had not felt since he had left his mother's side.

## Stage 2, Step 2 – Tests and Trials

*(During this time the Hero is tested through the trials of life. It is by overcoming these tests that he gains strength. These Tests and Trials happen all the way through this Adolescent Stage of Growth. The rewards the Hero gains later are only possible because of the lessons he learns at this stage. People often talk about being in flow but in order to be in flow you have to have a free channel. Overcoming Tests and Trials unblocks the channel that creates flow.)*

He had not travelled far before he saw a pretty white castle laid to siege.

Up on the battlements a fair maiden with long blond hair and dressed in a white flowing gown looked sadly down at the scene below.

Parzival felt his heart soar at the sight of her and knew he must champion her cause. "Is this love?", he thought, like the poetry he had learned to read at his mentor's home.

Parzival urged his horse to a gallop and soon found himself in front of the gates of the castle facing the besieging army.

"Who is the leader here?" he called.

"I am, Duke Orilus. Who dares challenge me?"

"I do, Parzival, Lord of this Land. I have heard of you as a pitiless tyrant. By what right do you lay siege to this castle?"

"By right of arms," answered the Duke.

"Then fight me and let's settle whose arms are strongest, right here, right now," challenged Parzival.

"And why would I do that? The castle will be ours on the morrow. Why would I risk all to fight you?"

"Because Parzival of Wales will call you a coward if you do not. All your men for all time will know you for the weakling you are. Throughout the lands they will spit when you pass and in the taverns they will laugh at the mention of your name."

Orilus looked around at his men. Already he could see them nodding and some even daring to smile.

## STAGE 2 – ADOLESCENCE – CROSSING THE FIRST THRESHOLD

"Come at me then," Orilus cried, as he shut his visor and galloped towards Parzival with his lance ready to strike.

Parzival lowered his visor and galloped to meet his opponent. The lances shattered on the shields and soon the two men had staggered to dismount and engage in swordplay.

Orilus was a mighty warrior and swung his sword in heavy arcs. Parzival bided his time, nimbly dancing out of the older man's way and waiting for the right opportunity to strike.

"Come fight like a man," Orilus cried.

"You fight like a beast not a man," retorted Parzival.

This made Orilus even more furious and for a while his blows were struck with renewed vigour. Parzival took many on his shield and found them reverberating down his arm and into the depth of his soul.

But Parzival also noted that the older man was tiring, while his inflated pride was making him reckless.

Then the moment came; the momentum of his assault unbalanced Orilus. Parzival raised his sword and smashed the Duke's visor off his head.

Orilus staggered and fell and Parzival stood over him with his sword point at his throat.

"Yield," Parzival cried.

"Kill me instead, there is nothing left for me now."

"No," Parzival cried. "There has been enough death and killing on my lands. Your greed has caused you to forfeit your titles. In exchange for your life, go to Arthur's court where I have heard your daughter still lives. Let the King know that Parzival of Wales is a true and worthy knight."

"Very well, Parzival. You have bested me and I will do as you command, though it dishonours me to do so."

"As you would have dishonoured the fair lady on the castle walls. Go and seek redemption. I will have no more war and if I kill you, no doubt someone else will come looking for revenge."

Then Parzival turned to the cheering from the castle walls and the radiant smile from the lady who was now at the open castle gates.

To the men at arms he cried: "You are now the men of this fair lady and hers to command."

## Stage 2, Step 3 – Meeting the Goddess
### Principle of Creativity, Secret of Imagination

*(Although Parzival is able to overcome Orilus there are a whole set of Parzival's Tests and Trials he cannot overcome with skills and knowledge alone. By meeting the Goddess Parzival is introduced to love. Blanche Fleur's love allows Parzival to go through another process of maturation. Through her understanding and nurture he is able to overcome his mother's restrictions and fears that he has still been carrying with him. Together they can imagine a future together and create a prosperous kingdom.*

*This is not the end of Parzival's Tests and Trials. He has more to face but Meeting the Goddess provides a new way of seeing the world that he did not possess before and new resources that he could not receive from his male mentor.)*

The lady smiled. "Come, those who were once enemies will now be friends. Sir Knight, I am Blanche Fleur the ruler of this castle and if it pleases you, you are our honoured guest."

That night Parzival feasted in the castle walls. The people, who had been starving and about to surrender, were now fortified by the stores of the invading army.

Parzival and Blanche Fleur sat at the head of the table, exchanging shy smiles and stilted conversation.

Finally, Blanche Fleur coyly said: "As our saviour, you can claim my hand in marriage. Would that please you Parzival?"

"With all my heart, Blanche Fleur, but one such as you should not be a

## STAGE 2 – ADOLESCENCE – CROSSING THE FIRST THRESHOLD 159

spoil of war. I can see that you sacrificed a great deal along with your people and that your heart is as pure as your beauty is bright."

"I thank you kind sir, but nothing would please me more than to spend my life with you. In so short a time you have become the knight of my heart."

And so the two were married. They saw no reason to delay and it pleased the people to have something to celebrate after all their suffering.

The night of the wedding Blanche Fleur and Parzival stood finally alone in the bridal chamber.

She was only wearing a white shift and slid into the bed. Parzival took off his wedding finery but underneath still wore the filthy remnants of the clothes his mother had made for him. Then he also slipped into the bed.

Blanche Fleur found this surprising but her love was great enough to overcome the discomfort of his odd dress, foul smell and strange behaviour.

Then, remembering his mother's words, Parzival gave Blanche Fleur a chaste kiss and rolled over to go to sleep.

Staring at his back, Blanche Fleur could feel hot tears pooling in her eyes. She had been strong right through the siege but this was meant to be the happiest day of her life and the man she loved was rejecting her.

In her modesty, she did not know what to do but go to sleep. The next morning she found herself still a maid and the morning after that as well.

By the third night she could stand it no more.

"Do I not please you, my love?" she timidly asked. "Perhaps you felt forced into a marriage by convention and do not love or want me."

Parzival turned in surprise. "No, my love. You are the light of my heart. Why would you think I love you not?"

"We are married now, Parzival. Although I do not know much about such things, I do know that it is normal to make love to one whose love has been consecrated by holy vows. Yet you still wear your sackcloth like a monk and I am still a maid."

A wave of confusion crossed Parzival's face. "My mother told me for love of her to never take off these clothes I wear. She also said that to all women I can only give a chaste kiss and perhaps a ring. You have the ring and the chaste kiss, what more should I do?"

Suddenly, Blanche Fleur realised it was Parzival's innocence and not his dislike of her that caused the rejection.

"Oh my love, your mother just sought to protect her boy, but you are now a man. Nay, not just a man but a knight. You are the champion of my heart and we are married. Come let me help you take off these clothes and bathe."

With her own hands Blanche Fleur helped Parzival take off his mother's remnants. She washed his body till it shone pink and clean as it had not for many, many months.

Then she led him back to bed and opened her arms to his embrace. In their bodies there awoke such a tender passion that Blanche Fleur blossomed like the flower she was and Parzival found a new form of swordplay.

When they awoke the next morning they felt a joy they could not put into words. When they entered the court their faces painted a picture of happiness and contentment that was clear for all to see.

In the months to come the city and countryside were repaired and Parzival marvelled at his good fortune. He felt his prayers had been answered and wondered at how wrong his mother could be.

When he mentioned this to Blanche Fleur she said: "But it seems sad that she is alone in the forest. Perhaps you could send for her."

"I fear her mind is such that she would trust no one but myself. I do think I should seek her and bring her to our happy home," said Parzival.

"Well go then and find her," said Blanche Fleur with a generous heart, little knowing what her kindness would cost her.

# STAGE 2 – ADOLESCENCE – CROSSING THE FIRST THRESHOLD

Parzival set out the next day. The sky was overcast and a great mist covered the land and after many hours riding, he realised he was lost.

He passed by a great lake where a man in rich clothing was busy fishing.

"God protect you, sir." Parzival called across the lake.

"And you too," came the answer in a voice laced with pain.

"I am weary from my travels. Is there anywhere to rest in these parts?"

The Fisherman directed him down the road. There Parzival found a great castle.

"Who goes there?" cried a voice from the battlements.

"I am Parzival of Wales and the Rich Fisherman on the lake bid me find refuge here," he answered.

"If the Fisher King sends you then you are welcome at Montsavage."

The gates opened and Parzival was offered a bath and refreshments before the hours passed and it was time for dinner.

At dinner before a roaring fire the Fisher King lay reclining on a bed.

"Forgive me if I do not rise," the King said in obvious pain. "Come and sit beside me."

## Stage 2, Step 4 – Temptation Failed

*(Parzival is being tempted to stay in Adolescence and he actually fails the test – by obeying his mentor's words instead of following what he really thinks is the right thing to do.*

*In this way Parzival avoids taking responsibility for his actions. Later he can blame the training he gained for his failings instead of his own lack of judgment. After all, his teacher taught him lessons in a particular context in an attempt to curb Parzival's incessant questions that were a reflection, in many ways, of Parzival's insecurities. Once he has left Gurnemanz he needs to follow his own judgment. Here he is tempted to remain a student instead of becoming a compassionate man. He is more worried about how he appears than another's pain and in this way he remains a teenager.)*

Parzival was about to ask the Fisher King what ailed him but he remembered his mentor's words and thought it was best to hide his ignorance and ask no questions.

The two men stared at each other for a long moment. The older man wincing now not just with pain but also with disappointment.

At that moment a messenger arrived carrying a sword. "Sire, your niece bade me bring you this sword; she asked you to bestow it on someone worthy."

"Our guest shall have the sword," he said gesturing at Parzival.

"Sire, I couldn't possibly accept such an expensive present, I am a stranger to you."

But the Fisher King waved away his protest and Parzival found himself in the possession of a rare gift.

Then the doors opened and a page entered carrying a spear from which gouts of blood flowed. Parzival was astonished but again decided to keep his mouth shut.

Next, two women entered carrying candles in great gold candlesticks, other maids followed these with knives and forks and empty silver dishes and cups.

Finally, the last maiden entered more beautiful than all the rest. In her hands she carried a large chalice in which lay that radiant stone that men call the Holy Grail.

The moment the Grail was placed on the table, the dishes filled with the most delicious smelling food and the cups filled with wine.

"Eat, son," said the Fisher King. Parzival was famished and the food looked amazing and so he ate with gusto. The moment his plate emptied it magically filled again until he could eat no more and was fully satisfied.

Parzival wanted to ask questions of the great mystery of the Grail but again his fear of ridicule stopped his mouth. His mentor Gurnemanz's words still rang in his ears: "Remember, Parzival," he had said, "a wise knight never reveals his ignorance."

So after the meal silence fell and Parzival again found himself staring into the older man's red-rimmed eyes. The Fisher King grimaced in pain and anguish which Parzival witnessed but said nothing.

Then with a voice filled with dispair the Fisher King said: "Perhaps you are tired from your journey and would like to retire?"

With nothing more to say Parzival made his excuses and went to bed.

When he awoke, the castle was cold and empty. His clothes were neatly folded on the end of his bed and his armour stacked against the wall.

He dressed and wandered the castle and called out but it was now as deserted as a ruin. With his skin crawling with unease he went outside and found his horse saddled and ready to go.

He mounted and now eager to leave, headed for the outer gates of the castle.

As he passed under the archway he heard a haunting call. "Cursed sleeper! Have you no compassion? Could you not ask the question?"

"What question?" Parzival shouted, the hair bristling on the back of his neck and his horse dancing in circles.

"Too late now, fool. You forfeit all. Our land, our king, our hopes wither because of your pride."

Before Parzival's horse could take a further step away the castle vanished into the mist and he found himself all alone again by the great lake.

With his mind full of questions he could not answer, Parzival spurred his horse on and away from an unnamed shame that lingered in the air.

By nightfall, Parzival began to feel that the terrain was somehow familiar.

He rode to the top of the crest of a hill to see the fair castle of Caerleon stretched before him. Disturbed by the day's events, he thought that maybe this would be a fairer place to stay the night.

He may even salvage his wounded pride by claiming the knighthood he had once been promised all that time ago.

When Parzival entered the castle gates in his red amour and his horse with its flame red mane, he was instantly recognized and welcomed.

Immediately he was presented to King Arthur in front of the whole court.

"Last time you were here we treated you ill," said the King. "We did not recognise you for the true knight you were. Stories have reached us far and wide of your great achievements, not least the rescue of the fair Blanche Fleur, who I understand is now your wife."

"That is so, Sire. All I do I do for her and God," said Parzival humbly.

The court and the King clapped and cheered.

"When you were little more than a boy, you wished to be a knight. Is that still a desire you would like fulfilled?" asked the King.

"Only if you think me worthy," Parzival quietly answered.

"Well then, Parzival of Wales, kneel."

Parzival knelt and King Arthur drew his mighty sword, Excalibur, from its scabbard. The steel sang as it was withdrawn and the sword seemed filled with a light of its own.

Parzival closed his eyes in anticipation of the sword's light touch on his shoulder, when all of a sudden the air reverberated with a screeching shout.

"Arthur, Arthur!" called the voice.

Parzival opened his eyes and turned his head to see the most hideous woman he had ever seen. She rode a bony mule towards him and the King, and her face looked like the mask of a boar, with a pug nose and jutting tusks.

"Who dares defile the sanctity of this knightly ceremony?" cried the King in anger.

"I, Cundrie the Sorceress, say that only honourable Knights should sit at the Round Table, not cowards and fools."

## STAGE 2 – ADOLESCENCE – CROSSING THE FIRST THRESHOLD

"This man Parzival is honourable and deserves to be knighted. He killed the Red Knight who was terrorising our kingdom, he saved Blanche Fleur from the horrors of invasion and tamed the Baron Orilus and spared his life," said the King. "Besides he follows God's light and has won many other honours. He rules with Blanche Fleur, who is now his wife, with justice and dignity."

"Do you think me monstrous, oh King?" replied Cundrie. "This man who is fair of face is more wretched than I. He slew the Red Knight without warning with a javelin to his eye. Yet what is worse is that the Red Knight was of his own blood. Parzival is a kin slayer."

Parzival stared at Cundrie in dismay. He went to open his mouth but she shouted.

"Keep your mouth shut, fool, because it opens when it should not and yet when it should ask questions it remains shut. Was there not a question you should have asked?"

Parzival felt like he was living a nightmare, the very place where he sought redemption and honour had become the place of his greatest shame. Yet he still did not understand why.

Seeing him dumbstruck Arthur demanded, "Speak plainer, Madam".

"Then you shall know the truth," she declared. "This wretch has been in the presence of the Holy Grail and eaten of its bounty. But when the Fisher King, grimaced with pain and was tortured by his wound, this unfeeling fool did not ask any questions of compassion. So now because of him, the Fisher King and all his people continue to suffer and the land still lies in waste."

There was a shocked silence in the court.

In a strangled voice Parzival murmured: "But I did not know…I wanted to ask but…"

"But what, idiot?" Cundrie asked.

"But I was told by one who was as a father to me not to ask questions," gasped Parzival.

"Are you a child?" scoffed Cundrie. "Are you still in swaddling clothes? Can you not think for yourself? Is your heart made of stone? Or did the Fisher King not suffer enough for your liking? But what can one expect from a man who caused his own mother's death."

Parzival reeled in shock. "My mother?"

"You are not fit to call her such. Yes she died as you rode away and you did not have the heart to turn your head in farewell. If you had you would have seen her collapse and been able to help her. Instead she died alone on the forest floor in sight of her faithless son."

Parzival withdrew further into himself trembling with shock and horror.

"Is there anything that can be done?" Arthur asked quietly into the ensuing silence.

"For the mother, no, nothing brings the dead back to life," was Cundrie's blunt reply. "For the Fisher King and his land, only one who finds the Grail and asks the question can heal the pain."

Finally, Parzival found his voice and clinging onto this last hope cried: "I will go back there, I will find Montsavage and the grail. I will not fail the test again."

"Hah! A fool's errand! The Grail cannot be found by one who seeks it. That is one of its mysteries. You threw away your only chance."

"Nevertheless, I will not return home to the arms of my sweet Blanche Fleur until I have found the Grail and heal the king and his land."

With that Parzival left that Hall of Shame, mounted his horse and galloped out of the castle and into the wilds beyond the walls.

Parzival searched and searched for the Holy Grail to no avail. A year passed and then another and another; he fought furious battles and proved himself countless times.

To the world he had become the greatest knight, but even though he had renown, to himself he remained tainted by shame and ridicule.

The respect and recognition he had desired had turned to ashes in his mouth.

## STAGE 2 – ADOLESCENCE – CROSSING THE FIRST THRESHOLD

Nothing he did, no favour he gained, no victory he sought, no honour he won, could erase the gutting sense of unworthiness he felt deep inside.

He missed Blanche Fleur with a hollow yearning that daily reminded him that he was truly alone in the world and deserved to be shunned.

One night he dreamt of Blanche Fleur crying in her cold bed.

"Why do you cry my love?" he whispered to her.

"The one I love has abandoned me and yet I wait for you still. I want to hate you but my heart bleeds with love," she cried. "Why have you rejected me? I was always true to you."

"But I am true to our love. I have never once betrayed you." He reached out ghostly hands to comfort her but they passed right through her. "It is for my love of you I cannot come home for I am unworthy."

"If you love me still come home, my love, my Parzival," she wept.

"I cannot until I find the Grail."

"What is the Grail and whom does it serve?"

"I do not know my love," Parzival answered hopelessly.

"Then it is your own pride you seek not the Grail," she cried. "Do you love me less than your pride?"

"No my love…" but before he could say more she disappeared into the mists of his mind.

Was it true? Was it just his pride he sought to heal? Around him nature was a wasteland and this too was a reflection of the wounded Fisher King. Whom should he serve – the love of his wife or the blighted land and his oath? Had he not sworn an oath to Blanche Fleur as well?

He felt wretched. The world that had once seemed so simple had become complex and confused. He felt a despair so deep he could no longer rest. He mounted his faithful horse but had nowhere to go, so he let the reins go slack and the horse find his own way.

Without direction the horse plodded deeper and deeper into the dark woods.

The leaves grew dense and shunned the light.

The Dark Night of the Soul descended on Parzival, while his tortured mind twisted and turned. The noble beast he rode plodded on.

In the very deepest part of the forest Parzival's mind registered a shaft of sunlight penetrating the gloom. Kneeling in its rays was an old hermit praying.

The sight distracted Parzival, and from habit he said, "God Protect you, old man."

"And you, Sir," said the old man, opening his eyes calmly. "A good greeting on this Good Friday."

"Ah, the day when God died. But no matter, I spoke out of habit, for I believe in no God," replied Parzival wearily.

"Not even a God who died for your sins and was reborn," the Hermit replied, with irony rather than offence.

"If you knew the world as I do you may doubt that, old man," replied Parzival.

"I know something of the sorrows of this world and its temptations," the old man replied. "I think you have fallen into one of the worst of them."

## Stage 2, Step 4 – Temptation Overcome

*(Parzival is tempted to remain the injured adolescent who blames others for his mistakes and failings of character. He is tempted to hold onto his pride instead of seeing himself without excuses or excessive judgment. With the Hermit's help he can overcome temptation and step into the Young Adult Stage of Growth where he learns from his mistakes, takes responsibility for his failings and grows. For all of us this is such a huge psychological step, but when we take full responsibility for ourselves, our decisions and our actions, this is the moment we become truly free.)*

"And which is that?" asked Parzival, but he was hardly able to endure any more accusations.

## STAGE 2 – ADOLESCENCE – CROSSING THE FIRST THRESHOLD

"I mean despair," said the Hermit, "which is the injured face of pride."

"Or perhaps it is the only sane response to a world where nothing makes sense and innocence, belief and love are punished," Parzival retorted. "I ask you what kind of God makes a world such as this? Can you not see the suffering that surrounds you? Or have you simply escaped into the safety of darkness, so you cannot see?"

"I may be in the darkness of the forest but it is light here compared to the darkness of your soul, Sir Knight."

"I am the darkness, Sir Hermit."

"The darkness can be a great healer and teacher," said the Hermit. "Maybe it is time to unburden your mind and shed some light in the forest of your soul. For there is no suffering so great that it cannot be shared, and the load lightened."

"I was obedient to those I loved, I followed God's light and it led me here to the darkness," said Parzival.

"Let me ask you this, Sir Knight," the Hermit asked gently. "How can you know God's light if you do not know yourself? And how can you know yourself if you only do what others tell you?"

"But the man who advised me was my friend and like a father to me."

"The soul has its own path and it may ask you to do the very opposite of what your friends advise," said the Hermit. "How can we truly become adults if we repeat only the patterns of our parents? They lived their life for their times, we must live our life for ours. It is not for you to repeat your father's life but rather to grow into your own."

"I knew my father not, he died before I was born," Parzival replied, puzzled.

"And yet even in death his life rules your own," the Hermit replied. "The world is not a simple place where the rules of childhood can be applied when we become adults. There is not a simple path of light to follow."

"Mine was," Parzival replied quietly. "Everything was simple; the rules applied to all, not one rule for the world and another for me. Everything was as clear as the love I bear my wife. I long for such simplicity and innocence again, everything else just corrupts the heart."

"We were all born innocent, my friend," sighed the Hermit. "That is not the challenge. The true quest is to find the light inside the disappointments and pain. That is the true work of the soul and marks the difference between a man and a boy."

"What do you mean?" asked Parzival.

"It is not the infatuation of gaining the goal that is the true mark of a man. It is who he becomes when he cannot fulfil his heart's desire that is the mark of distinction. Does he fall into despair like a child crying over a toy that has been taken from him? Or does he search for the resilience that comes from knowing that there is a quest beyond the constant chasing after external gratification?"

"But I cannot rest until I have found the Grail," countered Parzival.

Suddenly, he saw the Hermit stiffen.

"No one comes before the Grail unless it is their destiny," said the Hermit. "This I know for I have seen it with my own eyes."

The Hermit now had Parzival's full attention and he felt hope surging through him as he had not felt for many a year.

"You know of the Grail?" cried Parzival, "you must tell me, what is it?"

For a moment the Hermit hesitated and then with a weary look said: "It is something sacred that was brought to earth from heaven by the Neutral Angels."

"The Neutral Angels?" Parzival asked.

"Yes, in heaven long ago there was a great war between the Angels of Light and the Angels of Darkness. The whole of heaven and earth was being torn apart by their struggle for dominion. But there were some who would not take sides in the terrible war. They were the Neutral Angels and they strove to hold the universe together. It was the Neutral Angels who brought the Grail to the earth."

"But what is it?" interrupted Parzival.

## STAGE 2 – ADOLESCENCE – CROSSING THE FIRST THRESHOLD

"It is the Stone of Healing that makes those who touch it whole."

"A stone," Parzival gasped, "from Heaven?"

"Yes and in that stone is wedded the virtues of both light and darkness. From that holy union flows all the bounty of the earth."

"If that is so then why are we surrounded by a wasteland? Why is the Fisher King still wounded?" asked Parzival.

"Because he was the Guardian of the Sacred Stone and yet he betrayed the Grail. So it is kept from us and he cannot be healed by it. That is until one who is as a son comes to the Grail Castle and has compassion for the sins of the father. For that to happen that man must ask a question of the King, that seeks to understand his pain," explained the Hermit sadly. "I did hear that there was one who could have brought restoration but he did not have the wits to ask the question."

Parzival's heart sank. Was there nowhere he could escape from his shame?

He took a deep breath and confessed: "I was that one. I was in the presence of the suffering King and failed to ask the question. Do you not see what a fool God has made of me. Do you now understand?"

"You!" The Hermit gasped. "Dear God this is cause for great sorrow indeed. What is your name, Sir Knight?"

"It is Parzival," he said.

"Parzival, my sister's son!" exclaimed the Hermit. "I am your uncle and the Fisher King is your father."*

"My father?" asked Parzival incredulous. "But my father is dead. Died in war as a knight, that is why my mother stole me away to the forest."

"Not dead," said the Hermit, "but mortally wounded; without the Grail he would have died. Its grace keeps him alive but cannot heal him."

"My God, I am fortune's fool!" cried Parzival. "I have fought countless knights and none have been found worthier but still I am not worthy of the Grail."

"You are proud and skilled but the Grail asks for more."

"But I have sacrificed my whole life to her," Parzival exclaimed in fury.

"You have done only what serves your pride and desire for recognition. The real quest you have failed," countered the Hermit

"What quest is that?" asked Parzival defensively.

"The quest inside. You see only your own virtues and blame all your miseries on the world outside."

"Not without reason," snapped Parzival. "For I have done nothing to deserve this fate."

"You will never find your light until you have explored your shadow and the shadow cast by your family. This is your internal quest to discover and heal."

Parzival sat in stunned silence; the Hermit continued:

"I heard once that the soul chooses the family to be born into and your body as well, whether that is true or not makes no matter. In order to be truly ourselves we need to heal the negative influence of our family and use those learnings to strengthen our soul. To be wholly ourselves we must admit our darkness and channel our light. The one we learn from the other guides our path. We must strive to embrace and love both as the stone from heaven does and from this union all healing comes."

Parzival looked down at his sword and saw how his mind had divided him from his heart and the contemplation of his soul, while his body pursued action. He thought about the painful despair this had caused him and compared that to the calm serenity of the Hermit in front of him. The Hermit was a veteran of pain and yet he had found peace.

"Come nephew," said the older man, "I pray, leave the world of action for a time and let's contemplate these things in friendship."

Parzival stayed what seemed like an age but was probably just one passing of the moon through its cycle. After his inner journey, he felt that life had meaning again, and simple things he used to take for granted, became an everyday wonder.

**STAGE 3**

# YOUNG ADULT – CROSSING THE SECOND THRESHOLD, APOSTASIS – DEATH AND RESURRECTION

*(Parzival dies to who he thought he was and is reborn to who he will become. He is no longer a naïve child and adolescent. He now knows the truth about who he is and what he has done. When previously he heard Cundrie's relentless criticism he realised what he had done but he was not ready to take responsibility for his actions, particularly those done in ignorance.*

*Through Cundrie he had however discovered his real purpose and that was to find the Holy Grail, which was actually his birthright and from there be reunited with his wife. Parzival no doubt felt that meeting Cundrie was the worst thing that had ever happened to him but in fact she was the nemesis he needed in order to find his true identity and test his metal. This is the case with so many of us. Often the worst experience becomes the making of us. As the months and years drag on however he finds the near impossible task of finding the elusive Grail takes its toll and he falls into the biggest temptation of all, despair.*

*Finally with the Hermit's help Parzival overcomes his despair. He realises that life is not black and white and that moral dilemmas are everywhere. In some ways his despair is a kind of mourning for the naïve child he once was. As he lets go of the part of the child ??her?? his teenage angst also disappears and he begins to truly take responsibility for himself in order to become a man.*

*Parzival finally dies to who he was, the teenager who was not mature enough to be the Grail Champion and is resurrected as the Grail Guardian.*

*In this way he becomes responsible for both his light and his shadow and therefore understand and accept that in others.*

*He no longer clings to the excuse of ignorance and embraces the lessons of experience and pain.*

*Just like Jesus died on Good Friday as an ordinary man to be reborn on Easter Sunday as a divine being, King of Heaven and Earth, so Parzival dies as an aspirant to become the Grail King.)*

Then one day Parzival knew it was time to rejoin the world. He bade the Hermit farewell and soon found himself again on a path with a destination he did not know.

Before he could climb the next rise Parzival heard a familiar shrill cry, "Parzival! Parzival." At the top of the hill was his old nemesis, the Sorceress Cundrie.

He rode to meet her, no longer afraid of her or the shame she had brought him.

"So Parzival, is your life yet free of sorrow?" she asked as her mule met his charger.

"Not yet, Cundrie," he answered. "For I still have not found the Grail and until I do, as you know, I have sworn not to see my wife."

"Your circumstances are the same and yet you are much changed," she said.

"I have learnt patience from the Hermit in the Woods," he informed her.

"Oh, so do you obey him now?"

"I am less a simpleton of light as I once was," Parzival smiled at her. "I know that although others may advise, the only direction I can truly follow is the one that comes from my own heart and what I make of my experiences."

"Even the difficult ones?"

"Yes, the difficult ones as well as the ones that bring happiness and love."

"Then you have grown wise indeed," she responded. "Perhaps the battles, ordeals and pain you have experienced were necessary for you to become the person who can obtain the Grail. Maybe the Grail does not hide itself from us but it is we who refuse to see."

"I would see it now with all my heart," answered Parzival, "but I know that when I am ready then the path will be revealed."

"Then come with me, there is one more challenge for you to overcome," she said and led him to the rise of the hill.

## Stage 3, Step 1 – God the Father, the Power
### Principle Order, the Secret of Insight

*(Often at this point in time the Hero faces his real father but it can simply be a metaphor for facing his greatest challenge or something that has enormous power. Here Parzival faces his greatest opponent. The power and strength he relied on in his sword shatters and he has to discover a new order, one not based on might but rather on wisdom and insight. His opponent recognises that Parzival is worthy of mercy and is also sure that Parzival would offer him the same honour. A new order begins, one that combines the masculine strength and feminine understanding just like the Grail Stone combines both light and dark. These are now no longer seen as good and bad but rather necessary partners for growth and regeneration.)*

"See that knight?"

"I do but I do not recognise his banner," Parzival replied. "Is he a Saracen?"

"He is," she replied. "And he stands between you and the Grail you seek."

"Dear God, Cundrie," he looked at her wearily. "Is there no end to the fighting?"

With a heavy heart Parzival urged his charger on to face the foreign knight. When they came close Parzival shouted, "What are you doing here Saracen?"

"I seek my father," the Saracen replied.

"A noble cause but you stand in my way, for I seek the Grail and cannot rest until I come into her presence again," cried Parzival.

"And you are in my way too, Christian," came the defiant reply.

Both men lowered their visors and charged. They were equally strong and having smashed their lances on the first attack had soon dismounted to fight with swords. Both were sure and quick, and the clash of arms ate up the hours as neither man gave way.

Then Parzival seeing a weakness in the Saracen's defences lifted his sword to strike. The sword given to him by the Fisher King flashed blue and red in the fading sunlight.

He brought the sword down on a gap in the Saracen's armour but as it struck it shattered into a thousand pieces.

The Saracen Knight was shocked but soon recovered and brought his own sword to rest at Parzival's throat. Parzival closed his eyes and on his lips there played a wry smile of acceptance. At last there would be no more fighting, no more killing, no more questing after elusive grails that could not be found. He breathed in a soothing breath of peace and found that nothing separated the world within him from the world without.

But there was no blow. Parzival opened his eyes and stared into the eyes of his opponent. Then he took off his helmet and said: "Before you finish me, let me know your name, Sir Knight. I have never been bested."

"You fought well, Christian," the Saracen Knight declared. "If your sword had not shattered, it would be me at your mercy. There can be no talk of victor and vanquished between us."

The Saracen Knight sheathed his sword and to Parzival's amazement offered him his arm to help him to his feet.

"You are a noble knight then," said Parzival as he took the Saracen's arm and was pulled to his feet. "What is your name?"

At that moment Cundrie, who had watched the fight, moved closer. "This man is Feirefiz Angevin, your brother," she declared. Then she turned to Feirefiz. "Take off your helmet and show your face to your brother."

## STAGE 3 – YOUNG ADULT – CROSSING THE SECOND THRESHOLD

In amazement, Feirefiz lifted his helmet. What Parzival saw there was his own reflection except his brother's face was dappled black and white.

"You are both your father's sons but by different queens, both of whom were injured by your father's pride. Without him, Parzival, you would never reach the Grail; he is the missing part of yourself. That was your last battle," she said to him smiling.

"The time for the sword is over," Cundrie declared as she disappeared in a shimmer of light but her voice lingered in the air and echoed, "it is the Grail that calls you now."

Parzival, who had been so close to death, now felt a bright new world open before him. In front of him he recognised the path to the Grail Castle, as if it had been there all along though he could not see it.

"This is the path to the Castle of the Grail", he said to his brother.

"If it pleases you I should like to come with you and see this wonder," said Feirefiz.

"The Guardians of the Grail are your family too and our father awaits us there," said Parzival.

"Our father?" Feirefiz said in wonder.

"Yes, he is the Fisher King now and his festering wound causes the land to lie in waste."

"Then it is time we were reunited with him, brother."

Parzival and Feirefiz walked side by side leading their horses beside the lake and recounted their adventures. Soon before them the Grail Castle rose out of the landscape surrounded by the still, reflective moat.

The drawbridge was raised and a voice called from the battlements: "Who dares approach the Castle of the Grail?"

For a moment Parzival hesitated; could he really be readmitted to the Castle that had been the place of his failure and shame. Then he remembered he was not the only one who had failed the Grail or who had been wounded. He realised he was neither to blame nor blameless, neither light nor darkness but, rather, human. Inside him both light and dark were as one like the Grail itself.

"It is I, Parzival of Wales" he called out proudly. "It is my destiny to be a Guardian of the Grail, which once I failed but will not again. This is my brother, Feirefiz, who I have recently found and will not be parted from."

As if by magic, the drawbridge lowered and the brothers entered the castle together.

At the door of the great hall, the Hermit stood and welcomed Parzival with a warm embrace. He then ushered the brothers into the presence of the Fisher King.

"Father," Parzival cried as he ran to the Fisher King's side, but a grimace of extreme pain crossed the old king's face and Parzival slowed his pace and sat gently down beside him. His eyes caught those of his father and his heart filled with compassion.

"What ails thee my king?" he whispered with tears swimming in his eyes as Parzival realised he had nothing to offer but his compassion. "What ails thee Father?"

In that tender question lay the essence of healing and it was as if the Grail Castle breathed a long-held sigh of relief. In that moment the Grail Maidens appeared with the Grail. Its healing light could finally reach and cure the Fisher King. The colour returned to his face and the wound closed and was magically healed.

## Stage 3, Step 2 – Achieving the Ultimate Boon
### Principle of Intuition, the Secret of Listening

*(Parzival's internal quest has allowed him to step into his true identity and really become a man. He has gained the necessary insight into others to be able to see their pain and have empathy.*

*He can listen to himself and use his intuition to ask the healing question of the Fisher King. He has matured enough to look past his own insecurities about 'getting it right' and his concerns about how he appears in order*

# STAGE 3 – YOUNG ADULT – CROSSING THE SECOND THRESHOLD

*to have true empathy for others. This opens up to him the gates to the Ultimate Boon and the Holy Grail appears and the Fisher King is healed. Next Parzival is reunited with his wife and the land regenerated.)*

Parzival and his brother turned and saw bands of light and darkness emanating from the Stone from Heaven and dancing.

"I see now," said Parzival to his brother, "that the Grail is like the earth surrounded by both light and darkness, which is the father and mother tp us all."

As the two brothers gazed in awe at the stone, its nature seemed to change. Instead of mineral brilliance it began to glow red and gently palpitate.

"Brother," whispered Feirefiz, "is the Grail not also like the human heart?"

"Yes, brother, it is, for who among us has a heart that does not dance with both light and shadow?"

Then before them the Grail changed again and became a womb where twin babies, one male and one female, floated in harmony. Then the children seemed to grow, and reflected in the surface of the Grail he saw his own face and that of his dear wife, Blanche Fleur.

## Stage 3, Step 3 – Refusal of Return

*(In this story the Hero does not have a Refusal of Return, this is quite common. Not every Hero goes through every single minor step particularly in the last stage of the Hero's Journey but all go through all the Archetypal Stages of Growth and major steps.)*

## Stage 3, Step 4 – Magical Flight

*(Blanche Fleur magically appearing is like a Magical Flight)*

He turned in wonder to see the eyes of his dear wife lost in the depths of his own.

"Welcome home, my love," said Blanche Fleur as her arms stretched out to touch his face. He clasped her hand and drew her into an embrace.

## STAGE 4

# MATURE ADULT – CROSSING THE THIRD THRESHOLD

*(Finally reunited with his beloved wife and having achieved all his goals and more, Parzival is finally a mature adult.)*

### Stage 4, Step 1 – Master of Two Worlds
### uses the Principle of Discernment, Secret Self-Love

*(Now that Parzival has become a mature adult he no longer has a child or adolescent desire to see things in black and white. He sees that every human heart is a dance of both light and shadow and he can love both for the resources and discernment they bring him. He has searched his shadow in order to heal and gain depth and experience. He has also embraced his light so he can achieve his goal while reconnecting with his wife. No longer does he need to sacrifice love to achieve, or sacrifice achievement for love. Now he can have both in harmony – he has truly become the master of two worlds.)*

### Stage 4, Step 2 – Freedom to Live
### uses the Principle of Results, Secret of Action

*(Parzival is now free to be who he truly is. He no longer needs to obey or rebel, nor does he need to be alone to follow his quest. He is free to finally fulfil his destiny and take his place as a Guardian of the Grail, as well as maintain and grow his relationship with his wife. Without taking internal action to heal his own pain and the external action to enter the Grail Castle and finally ask the Fisher King the question of compassion he would never have attained his destiny. We all need a balance of both internal exploration and healing and external actions and results to be successful and happy.)*

And so Parzival was reunited with his whole family. He was no longer wounded or lonely. Like the Grail, he had healed the rift between the light and darkness within his very soul. His restless heart could be at peace and he was truly able to love and serve.

Now was the time to bring order to the kingdom, for both his brother and himself would share the task of being the Fisher King and Parzival and Blanche Fleur would rule their own kingdom as well. There was much to do to restore the land but with the help of the Grail their task would always be successful and they were able to balance achievement, love and happiness in all they did.

## The End

Except of course when they, like you, are Called to the Next Adventure!

## WANT THE NEXT QUEST?

If you would like like more information or
continue your journey of transformation, then go to:

www.pipmckay.com

where you will find a wealth of videos and support materials.

# BIBLIOGRAPHY

Katie, Byron; *The Work of Byron Katie*. hhttp://the work.com/

Byrne, Rhonda; *The Secret*; 2006; Atria Books, USA

Campbell, Joseph: *The Hero with the Thousand Faces*; 1949; Pantheon Press. Third Edition, 2008; New World Library

Dr Case, Paul Foster: *The True and Invisible Rosicrucian Order*; 1981; Builders of the Adydum, 1985; Samuel Webster.

Coppens, Philip: Servants of the Grail, The Real-Life Characters of the Grail Legend Identified,

Clarke, Lindsay: *Parzival and the Stone from Heaven - a Grail Romance for Our Time*; 2002, Thorsons Publisher, 2009, O-Books, United Kingdom

Cameron, Julia: *The Artist's Way, A Spiritual Path to Higher Creativity*; 1997, Pan Books, London.

Dr Davies, Ann: Transcripts from Class Lectures, Developing Supersensory Powers; 1961, Builders of the Adytum, Los Angeles 42, California, USA

Dawkins, Peter: *The Shakespeare Enigma, Unravelling the Story of the Two Poets*: 2004, Polair Publishing London

Hall, Manly: *The Secret Teachings of All Ages*; 1972, 8th Edition, The Philosophical Research Society, Los Angeles, California, USA

Moyle, Franny: *Desperate Romantics: The Private Lives of the Pre-Raphaelites*; 2009, Julian Murray Publishers, UK

Hibbert, Christopher; *The Rise and Fall of the House Medici*; 1974 Christopher Hibbert; 1974, Penguin Group, USA

Hillman, James: *The Souls Code, In Search of Character and Calling*; 1996 James Hillman; 1997, Bantam, Great Britain

Jung, Carl; The Red Book Liber Novus; 2009, 1st Edition, Philemon Series, Switzerland

Rohn, Jim; *7 Strategies for Wealth and Happiness*; 1985 Jim Rohn; Three Rivers Press, 1996, USA

Einstein; Albert; Interview published in "The Saturday Evening Post" in 1929, Great Britain

Prof Snyder; Allan: Centre for the Mind, Sydney University, Pip's Personal Interview with him in 2001, Sydney, Australia

Shakespeare; William: *Romeo and Juliet;* 1975, Crown Publishers, USA

Three Initiates: *The Kybalion, A Study of Hermetic Philosophy of Ancient Egypt and Greece;* 1912, Yogi Publication Society

**Films**

Star Wars, The Lion King, The Matrix, Finding Nemo, Gone With The Wind, Lord of the Rings

# About Pip McKay

Pip McKay is a highly respected thought leader and pioneer within the field of personal transformation, coaching and NLP.

She has dedicated over 20 years of her life to creating techniques which allow you to discover your unique Passion and Purpose, remove negative influences and fulfill your true potential.

Pip is an exceptional speaker and extraordinary personal coach. She has created the entire field of Matrix Therapies® Coaching and Archetypal Coaching®. She is the CEO of *Evolve Now! Mind Institute Pty Ltd. and Archetype Academy®*.

Her proven techniques have been taught throughout Australia and internationally including most recently Israel. They are based on proven psychological, spiritual, historical and intellectual foundations, which create a holistic new movement in coaching.

Her students include award-winning actors, football stars, entrepreneurs and authors, as well as, ordinary people who want extraordinary lives.

Pip has also been influential within the corporate arena, training teams and executives in many organisations including Malleson's Law Firm, NRMA, MBF, Manhattan and the United Nations.

Just hearing Pip speak is transformational – attending training or coaching sessions is life changing.

Pip lives in Manly with her adored partner Will and loves animals, nature and the beach.

To contact her or gain more information go to www.pipmckay.com.au

www.ingramcontent.com/pod-product-compliance
Lightning Source LLC
Chambersburg PA
CBHW070615300426
44113CB00010B/1534